A MENTOR MANUAL

For Adults Who Work with Pregnant and Parenting Teens

by Frederick H. Kanfer, Susan Englund, Claudia Lennhoff, and Jean Rhodes

The Child Welfare League of America
Washington, DC

CHILD WELFARE LEAGUE OF AMERICA, INC.
HEADQUARTERS
440 First Street, NW, Third Floor, Washington, DC 20001-2085
E-mail: books@cwla.org

CURRENT PRINTING (last digit)
10 9 8 7 6 5 4 3 2

Cover and text design by Jennifer Riggs Geanakos

Printed in the United States of America

ISBN # 0-87868-580-4

Contents

Foreword ◆

As a new or expectant mother, your partner is probably going through the most challenging time in her young life. You are in a crucial position to help her make the most of these challenges and to guide her in taking healthy steps toward her future. With your help, your partner can develop the skills that she needs to work toward her goals. This manual can help you with that process. It is based on techniques and strategies that have been shown to help all sorts of people make positive changes in their lives.

You probably already know and use many of the ideas in the following chapters. Still, it may be helpful to find them gathered together in one place. Please take some time to read through the manual. Then, as problems and challenges arise in your relationship with your partner, you will be able to refer back to certain sections.

At the back of this manual you will find three sets of fact sheets. We encourage you to integrate information from these sheets with the strategies and techniques outlined in the 12 chapters. For example, when you deal with parenting issues, you might use the example of Tanya and her mother in chapter 7 and also share information about parenting from the After the Baby Is Born fact sheets.

Never forget, though, that the main ingredients in this relationship are you and your partner. We expect and encourage you to draw on your own wisdom and provide your own unique input throughout the mentoring process.

Acknowledgments

The authors are indebted to the mentors from the Bobby Wright Mental Health Center and the Simpson Alternative School Mentor Program for their wisdom, experience, and expertise in mentoring, which they generously shared with us.

Further, the authors would like to thank Ms. Doris Williams, Principal of Simpson Alternative School, without whom the Simpson Mentor Program would not have been possible.

Finally, we gratefully acknowledge the assistance of Preston M. Gazaway, III, M.D., Director of Women's Health Care, Total Health Care, Baltimore, MD, who reviewed the sections on pregnancy and infant care for accuracy and currency.

Pregnancy: A Time of Change

Whether a pregnancy is planned, unplanned, or somewhere in between, it is always a time of great physical and emotional change. For every woman, pregnancy brings a baffling range of new feelings—from nervousness to excitement to sadness and back again. For a pregnant teenager these feelings may be especially powerful and the experience of change especially confusing.

Changes for your partner

Changes in her life-style

If the pregnancy is unexpected, a teenage girl may feel she has lost control of her life. It may be hard for her to stay in school because she feels sick or can't keep her mind on her studies. Her friends or family or boyfriend may treat her differently; her boyfriend may even leave her. She will probably need to make some extreme changes in her life-style—for example, in her eating habits and in any use of alcohol, drugs, or cigarettes. She may feel sick and uncomfortable in her changing body, or she may even feel like her body has betrayed her by becoming pregnant. On the other hand, she may see this time as an opportunity to take charge of her life and make some changes she has been thinking about but just not gotten around to.

Changes in her body

The fact that she is young and her body has not finished with its own growth complicates matters further. For example, good nutrition, extremely important with any pregnancy, is even more important to a pregnant teenager because both her growing body and her baby's growing body need nourishment. Because most teenagers like fast food and snacks, her change to good nutrition may be especially difficult. A teenager may experience pregnancy complications due to her young age. She is also at risk for giving birth to a baby who is too small or too early. See the fact sheets on pregnancy for detailed information to help your partner.

Changes in her feelings

Chances are that your partner will go through a roller coaster of feelings and experiences during her pregnancy. At times she may be happy she is having a baby. At other times she may be unhappy. As she begins the long journey of pregnancy and parenting, she will have lots of questions and lots of decisions to make.

The good news is that teenagers are often open to making big changes in their lives during their pregnancies. Your partner will need to change her life-style to meet the needs of her growing baby before and after it is born. Partly, this means avoiding things that are harmful. It also means taking a good long look at her life and deciding how she wants to live it. This is her chance to take charge of her life.

How this manual can help

This manual will give you, her mentor, the tools you need to help her take positive control of her life and give her baby the best start it can have. In the pages that follow you will find ideas about how to help her build her self-confidence. One of the most important ways you can do this is to believe in her—believe she is strong enough and smart enough to make it. Tell her so, every chance you get, and show it through your actions. This manual will suggest some strategies for helping her learn to be self-reliant. When you treat her as a capable adult, she'll feel and act more and more like a capable adult. As she learns how self-sufficient she can be, her competence and confidence will grow.

She makes the changes

Always remember that she is the one who must make the changes. She must be willing to work to make her life better for herself and her baby. You, of course, will be there to help her—but you cannot do it for her. She must take responsibility for herself. This manual will help you to help her work toward the goals she cares about most. But she must achieve them for herself.

You help her learn to trust

One of the first and most important things you can do as a mentor is to actively build a relationship of trust with your partner. A strong trusting relationship with you will give her a chance to talk about things that are important to her. The sooner she learns to trust you, the more she will get out of your partnership. Then she will be willing to listen to you, to take your advice, and to feel truly supported.

One thing you can do to help her trust you is to express your confidence in her and your commitment to working with her. Give her this message: "I have confidence that you can do this—and I will be there to help when you need me."

For some girls, this may be the first time that anyone has expressed any confidence in their abilities or any interest in them for who they are. Knowing that someone believes in them can be a very empowering experience.

Although your partner might not trust you as much as you would like her to at first, chances are, with consistent support and genuine concern from you, she will begin to feel comfortable in time. You may find that she feels the need to test you, to see if she can rely on you to be there for her, to keep the secrets she asks you not to tell, and to accept her for herself. She might even do something she knows you won't like to see if you will still like her or will abandon the relationship. If this happens, you must make clear to her that you dislike what she did, but you still like her.

The Mentor-Partner Relationship: Lessons from Experience

Although you may begin your relationship with your partner with the best of intentions, these intentions are not always enough to guarantee success. With a little bit of foresight, however, many problems can be prevented before they ever begin. Problems that cannot be avoided or prevented can be worked through successfully. The purpose of this chapter is to prepare you for the kinds of problems you might encounter in your relationship with your partner. These suggestions for avoiding and dealing with problems in mentor-partner relationships came from the experience of other mentors who are working with teenagers.

Don't take it personally

Perhaps the biggest problem mentors face when they begin a relationship with their partner is unrealistic expectations. It's important to be prepared for setbacks. Your partner may act in ways that leave you feeling disappointed or hurt because you interpret her actions too personally. Here are three common examples.

Partner's lack of interest

The most common complaint from mentors is that their partners don't seem to be interested in them. In some cases, a partner may be not only indifferent but even hostile to her new mentor. Don't be surprised if your partner isn't talkative or responds to your questions with one-word answers. This can make it very difficult and awkward to hold a conversation, but as her mentor, it is important for you to be patient with your partner. Continue to spend time with her, understanding that she may be uncommunicative for a variety of reasons.

- She is reluctant to trust because she has been let down by other adults in the past.

- She may not be used to thinking that what she has to say is important, or that anyone cares about what she thinks.

- Adolescence is typically a time of rebellion against all adults.

Remember that even though your partner doesn't show it, your relationship may be extremely important to her.

Partner's lack of effort

At least in the beginning, your relationship may be very one-sided. Because you are the adult, more of the relationship work and responsibilities will naturally fall on your shoulders. But even knowing that, your feelings may get hurt if you think that your partner doesn't care enough to make an effort. At these times, remember that teenagers in general are not likely to make the same effort as adults. You will still receive the intangible benefits of the relationship, such as the satisfaction of knowing that you are helping your partner through a very difficult and challenging time in her life.

Difficulties staying in touch

Many mentors become upset when their partners fail to call them or return their calls. Partners may also forget appointments or meetings. Keep in mind that your partner probably does not have an appointment book to remind her of her schedule.

Some teens may not even have telephones. If this is the case, you will have to make special arrangements for contacting each other. Some mentors have arranged to have their partners call them at work or at home during the partner's lunch hour.

Here are some suggestions for keeping in touch with your partner:

- Make a plan to contact your partner at the same time each week to discuss your plans for that week.

- If your partner is not home when you call, do not assume that she will call you back, even if you leave a message asking her to do so. Call her back later or the next day.

Be patient

Schedule time together

Especially in the beginning of the relationship, it is very important to try to spend time together once a week on some activity. If this is not possible, then at the very least talk on the phone and try to schedule something for the next week. Most successful mentor-partner pairs do some activity together once a week that lasts for several hours. Later in the relationship, when you have established trust and good communication, you may be able to spend time just talking on the phone. In the early stages of the relationship, though, talking on the phone together is usually not very satisfying, since partners tend not to be talkative.

Trust and disclosure take time

Although you will be eager to get to know your partner well, it is important to remember that relationships are built over time and through a process of developing trust. Many mentors want their partners to be able to confide in them right away. Sometimes they even begin the relationship with this as their goal, and feel that they have failed if they do not become their partner's confidante right away. Mentors with these expectations are often disappointed when their partners don't talk about personal things.

Dwelling on problems may drive her away

As a mentor, you may want to tackle your partner's most personal problems right away. If she is not doing well in school, or if she is having problems in her relationship with a family member, you might be inclined to ask her questions about these things, and to think that you can help solve her problems by talking them through. Although your intentions are good, your partner may perceive your questions as intrusive, nosy, or even judgmental. As a result, she may choose to answer with as few words as possible, she may change the subject, or she may just ignore you altogether.

Do not view your partner's unwillingness to talk about these things as a sign that your relationship is a failure or that she doesn't like you. Instead, try to be patient and respect her need for privacy. If your partner withdraws from you because she feels pushed to talk about personal things, your relationship may never have a chance to develop to the point where she would voluntarily talk to you about these things.

There's more to talk about than problems

If your partner is reluctant to talk about her personal problems, it might not be because she doesn't trust you, but because she doesn't feel a need to talk about personal things. The kind of relationship she wants with you might be one where she doesn't have to talk about those things.

Don't worry if your conversations are not very personal. Having ordinary conversations is a good thing in itself. Perhaps she has no one to talk with about everyday things. As a pregnant or parenting teenager, she may need you to be someone she can have fun with.

Of course, it is still wise to be sensitive to any cues your partner may give that she would like to talk about something that is troubling her. Listen carefully for any openings she may give you to address more private matters. Then you can gently ask her questions. Depending on her response, you might find that she is willing to discuss some of the things that are troubling her. For techniques to help you talk about difficult things with your partner, see chapter 3, When Talking Is Hard.

Listen to your partner

Encouraging her to talk

Listening has been called the cardinal rule of mentoring. Although your partner may be quiet a lot of the time, this does not mean she doesn't have anything to say. You can show her that you are interested in what she has to say by asking her questions.

But listening is not just about asking questions and paying attention to the answers. Listening is about paying attention all the time, even when it seems like your partner is not saying anything important. Listen to the interests your partner expresses, even if they just seem like comments made in passing. These will give you ideas for activities that you can suggest doing together.

Sometimes it is difficult and frustrating to talk with a partner who isn't very talkative. Sometimes you might be tempted to talk just to fill the silence. One mentor described having to get used to the discomfort of silence, in order to avoid just rambling on whenever her partner was silent. The danger of this, of course, is that it can become a pattern of interaction. When the partner remains silent much of the time, and the mentor talks a lot, the partner's needs do not get communicated.

Emphasize the positive

Avoid being judgmental

Teenagers are very sensitive to criticism. Adolescence is a time of trying to establish independence and also of being acutely self-conscious. Your partner may be extremely sensitive to criticism or judgment.

If she tells you about something that is troubling her, try to really listen, whether you sympathize with her or remain neutral, and try to be supportive. You can be supportive by acknowledging her feelings and by not judging her. If she is trying to solve a problem, you can offer support by suggesting alternative solutions, rather than by pointing out what she did wrong or what to do next. She will probably appreciate your suggestions and your support.

Let her know that you enjoy her

Letting your partner know that you enjoy her company is a good way to establish communication and trust, and to move your relationship from one-sided communication to sharing. Tell-ing your partner that you enjoy spending time with her lets her know that she is giving something to the relationship. It is important for her to know that you are there because you genuinely enjoy her company, not just because she is someone who needs help. The relationship will have a better balance if she knows that she is important to you and that she has nice things to offer in a relationship.

Don't forget to have fun

Whatever you do, don't forget to have fun with your partner! It is easy to underestimate the importance of having fun together. While you may think that your partner needs to spend time talking about her problems, she may just want to forget her problems and do something fun for a change. If her baby is already born, she probably has very little time in her life to do things that she enjoys. Having fun together is a good way to build your relationship with your partner. Especially in the beginning, when conversation may be difficult, activities you share can give you something to talk about and a way of getting rid of nervous energy.

Choose varied and interesting activities

Mentors and partners do many different kinds of things together. Some pairs enjoy eating out together, going shopping, visiting a college or work setting, seeing a movie, cooking a meal together, or just hanging out at the mentor's home.

Even if you end up doing task-oriented activities with your partner, such as helping her find a job, you can still make sure there is room for fun. You can schedule time before or afterwards for eating out or going shopping.

Some things that seem ordinary or even boring to you might be very enjoyable to your partner. Many mentors have been surprised to find that their partners really enjoy being able to prepare a meal together. Although cooking may seem like a chore at times, it can be fun to do together, especially if your partner does not get to do this at home.

No matter what you do together, make sure that your partner has a role in choosing. You can suggest things you think might interest her on the basis of previous conversations or things that you have noticed about her.

Be sensitive to your partner's family

Over the course of your relationship with your partner, you may encounter some difficulties with her family members, with her boyfriend, or with other significant people in her life. This section will provide an overview of the kinds of problems you may encounter. No matter what the problem, the basic thing to remember is that as her mentor, you are responsible and committed primarily to your partner. She needs to be able to feel that you are there for her, and that she can confide in you without worrying that you will tell someone else what she has told you. In general, any relationships that you develop with other people in your partner's life should be more formal than your relationship with your partner; they should be established through your partner; and they should remain secondary to your relationship with her.

When family members feel threatened

Sometimes mentors report that a member of their partner's family feels threatened by her relationship with the mentor. When this problem arises, it typically involves the partner's mother. Perhaps she is uncomfortable about your relationship with her daughter if she feels that you are trying to take her place, or if she thinks you are there because she is doing a bad job as a mother.

If these feelings and fears are strong enough, the mother may try to disrupt the relationship you have with your partner. Sometimes mentors report that their partners' mothers have made it difficult for them to schedule time together, or even to keep in touch with each other. Disrupting the relationship can take the form of not telling the partner that the mentor called, or saying her daughter is not home when she really is. When mothers feel threatened, it is often helpful to involve them in the planning or to tell them about the benefits of the relationship.

This problem is not limited to the mothers of partners. Sometimes the partners' boyfriends or other friends also become very threatened and try to sabotage the relationship. They might feel that your partner spends less time with them because she's spending more time with you. Or, if she starts to change in any way, they might become alarmed and try to keep things as they were. People get used to relationships being a certain way, and it can be very scary when they start to change.

One mentor reported that her partner's boyfriend was trying to undermine the relationship. She and her partner had made special plans for a weekend evening. The partner was very excited, and she told her boyfriend about the plans. The boyfriend then invited the partner to go out with him on the same evening. She was very tempted by her boyfriend's offer because he typically never took her out. When difficulties with a boyfriend arise, you'll need to decide whether to work directly with him or through your partner to clear up any misunderstandings.

Try to prevent such problems from arising by getting to know the important people in your partner's life, especially family members like her mother. This can reassure them that you are not there to replace them and that they have not somehow failed the young woman. But be sure these connections never take priority over your relationship with your partner.

Apathetic or uninvolved families

Another difficulty you may encounter with members of your partner's family is apathy or indifference. Your partner's mother may be uninvolved and offer no support for your relationship with her daughter. The consequences may not be as serious as those from a threatened mother, but they may make it difficult for you and your partner to meet and spend time together. Again, even though it may be difficult, try to establish some kind of connection with the mother.

Over-involvement with family members

You might encounter quite a different problem with your partner's family. It sometimes happens that mentors become drawn into their partners' families and develop close relationships with other family members. Sometimes family members even want the mentor to mentor them.

It is difficult not to be drawn into this situation, especially if you feel that you can really help another person in your partner's family. Nonetheless, by helping her family members you may end up taking time and energy away from your relationship with your partner. In addition, close relationships with your partner's family members may compromise the trust and integrity of your relationship with her, because she may no longer feel that she can talk to you about family troubles or trust you with things she wouldn't want her family to know.

Again, it is simply best to maintain a comfortable distance from your partner's family members. Your partner really needs the benefits that come from having a supportive relationship with someone who is there especially for her.

To summarize

1. *Don't* take it personally. Your partner's difficulties in accepting your support probably have nothing to do with you.

2. *Do* be patient. Give your partner time to learn to trust you.

3. *Do* listen to your partner. Don't talk just to fill the silence.

4. *Do* emphasize the positive. Don't be judgmental. Relax and enjoy your partner's company.

5. *Don't* forget to have fun. Even activities that seem ordinary to you may be fun for your partner.

6. *Do* be sensitive to your partner's family. Reassure them if they are anxious, but remember that your primary responsibility is to your partner.

3 ◆ When Talking Is Hard

The most important first step in building a trusting relationship with your partner is to communicate with her. Trust is achieved through communication, so she needs to know that she can talk to you. You will probably have to be the one to open the lines of communication by talking to her and finding ways of letting her know she can talk to you.

Talking with a teenager can be hard. It is not always easy to know what to say or how to say it. Here are some suggestions that might help when talking to your partner is difficult. Some of these things you are probably doing already.

Show her you are interested

Before she will want to talk to you, your partner needs to know you are interested in what she has to say. You can show your interest in a number of ways. Looking at her when she is speaking and leaning forward are body language signs that show you are paying attention. Other things may be effective with your partner. You will be able to tell by her reactions what makes her most comfortable talking to you.

Some things you do or say while she is talking encourage her to go on. A lot of people do these things without even thinking about them. You probably do them too. Here are some examples of things that let people know you are listening to them and encourage them to go on:

- Paying attention
- Not interrupting
- Just listening—without thinking ahead to what you're going to say
- Asking questions to clarify what she has said
- Not giving unwanted advice or trying to change her feelings
- Nodding your head
- Saying things like "Mm-hm" or "Mmm" or "Uh-huh"
- Repeating a few words of what she has just said

You can encourage the conversation to move in different directions by repeating different parts of what she says. What she talks about next depends in part on what you say. You can help her focus on one particular part of her story by repeating the words she used that were most relevant to that part of the story.

Your Partner: When I go out with my friends they want me to drink—and even though I know I shouldn't, I almost give in because they push me to.

Mmm...

Uh-huh...

Mm-hm...

You: They push you to?

She: Yeah—they tell me it doesn't matter what I do now because I drank during the first month of my pregnancy anyway.

OR

You: You almost give in?

She: Yeah—I'm tempted but so far I haven't.

OR

You: Your friends?

She: Yeah—they just don't seem to get it. I don't think they're trying to hurt me or my baby, but they just don't understand.

Some things you do could make her think you are not listening or paying attention to her:

- Not looking at her

- Doing something else while she is talking

- Appearing to be distracted by other things that go on while she talks

- Changing the subject abruptly from what she was talking about to something else

Start the conversation and keep it going

Asking questions

Sometimes people have a hard time getting started talking about things. You can help to open up the conversation by using open questions.

Open questions

Open questions are questions that need more than a few words or yes or no as an answer. Open questions often start with words such as:

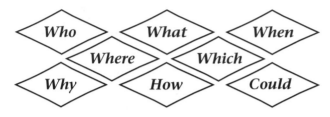

Who, what, when, where, and *which* are words that can help you gather more specific information about a situation.

- Who do you think you could talk to about this?

- What makes it so hard to eat the right foods?

- What do you mean by "he doesn't want to listen"?

- When will you find out the results of your tests?

- Where were you when all this happened?

- Which of those things were you most worried about?

How and *what* and *could* can help you get at details and feelings about a situation.

- How did it happen?

- What was going on at the time?

- Could you tell me more about what made you think that?

- What would you like to have happen now?
- How do you think you should handle this situation if it comes up again?
- Could there have been other reasons she acted that way?
- How did you feel when she refused to talk to you?

Why questions can get at reasons. Be careful, though. Why questions can make people feel defensive if they think you are questioning their judgment. When you use *why* questions, pay attention to how your partner is responding.

- Why did you think she was angry?
- Why did you do it that way?
- Why did you go there if you thought it might be dangerous?

Closed questions

Closed questions are questions that require only a yes or no answer. Sometimes this type of question can be useful, but sometimes, for instance if your partner is not very talkative, closed questions can be a conversation stopper. Closed questions start with words such as:

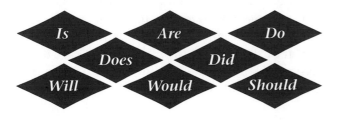

For example:
- Is there anything in particular you'd like to talk about today? (No.)
- Are you sure you don't want to talk about the fight you had with your girlfriend? (Yes.)
- Do you want to tell me what happened? (No.)
- Does your boyfriend's temper scare you? (No.)
- Did you go to school today? (No.)
- Will you remember to take your prenatal vitamins? (Yes.)
- Would you like to talk about how things are going? (No.)
- Should we talk about what happened yesterday? (No.)

Of course, both open and closed questions are useful in conversations. These tips about how your questions can change the way conversations turn out are meant as something for you to think about if you seem to keep hitting conversational dead ends.

Show that you understand what she's talking about

There are a lot of things you can do to let your partner know you are listening to her, hearing what she says, and understanding her. One thing you can do is to reflect back what she has said to you. Or you can reflect what you think she might be feeling—even if she hasn't come right out and said it. Here are some examples of things you can say that reflect what you've heard from her or what you think she might be feeling:

- It seems like you feel good about how you handled that situation.

- It sounds like you felt pretty upset when your sister talked about you like that.

- I imagine you feel worried by what the doctor said.

- You look angry.

- I'll bet that hurt.

Once you have opened up communication with your partner and she has begun to share her feelings with you, you may notice that she has many, and sometimes opposite feelings about the same thing. It is important to let her know it's normal to have mixed feelings.

Dealing with mixed feelings

Everyone has mixed feelings about someone or something. That's natural. Mixed feelings are especially common when there are lots of different angles on a situation. Your partner may have trouble sorting through her feelings, or she may feel conflicted and confused about a decision she's trying to make. These are the times when your partner will most need your help. There are some simple things you can do to help her.

Identify mixed feelings

Your partner may give you a variety of hints to tell you she is feeling mixed up about something. Sometimes she will simply say she has mixed feelings or she feels mixed up. She might say she is confused, or ambivalent, or upset. She might say she is feeling two or three different ways all at once. She might say she doesn't know how she feels. Statements like these tell you that your partner feels conflicted about something.

Find the different pieces

When someone has mixed feelings or is confused about something, she may find it helpful to identify the different things she is feeling. Sometimes people feel two things that are quite opposite from one another. By identifying and talking through her feelings, she will become less confused and be able to come to a decision more easily. Your role may be to help her figure out exactly what she is experiencing. Does she feel angry? Glad? Sad? Fearful? You can help her name her feelings by paying attention to the feeling words she uses. You can also ask her straight out—How do you feel about that?

Clarify feelings

There may be several different reasons why your partner has mixed feelings. She may actually have both good and bad feelings toward a person or situation at the same time. These feelings may confuse her. Asking her to tell you about her good feelings and her bad feelings separately can help untangle her confusion. It may also reassure her to point out that mixed feelings are a natural reaction. Most situations and people are not clearly all good or all bad.

Your partner may also experience mixed feelings because she is uncomfortable about having certain feelings. For example, she may feel bad about being angry at someone close to her. So, on top of feeling angry at someone, she may also feel guilty or uncomfortable about feeling angry. It may help for your partner to talk to you about all these feelings.

Point out that although they sometimes make us uncomfortable, feelings provide useful information. We often base decisions on how we feel. This is true of good feelings as well as bad feelings. If your partner feels uncomfortable about having a particular feeling, ask her what kind of information this feeling may be providing. Feelings provide us with cues about how to act, even when we can't put the reasons for having the feelings into words.

For example, your partner may feel distrustful of a male friend. Although at times she likes him, her feelings cause her to avoid spending time alone with him. She may feel bad because she can't explain why she doesn't trust him. The important thing is to understand that even though she can't explain it, her feelings tell her not to trust him. This provides her with the information that something about him makes her uncomfortable. Once you and your partner have sorted out her mixed feelings, you can help her explore where they come from and what they mean.

To summarize

1. Get tipped off by a mixed-feelings signal:
   - She uses more than one feeling word in talking about the same situation.
   - She uses words such as: *mixed up, confused, mixed feelings, upset, ambivalent.*
   - She doesn't know how she feels.
2. Help her identify the different and/or conflicting feelings she is having.
3. Help her clarify each of her positions one at a time.

Laying out all her positions and different feelings will equip your partner to make good decisions.

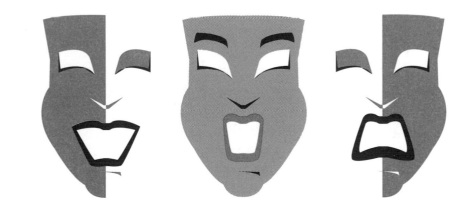

A Step In the Right Direction: "Think Rules"

In your work as a mentor, you may sometimes feel at a loss for what to do. The following six "think rules" can help you decide where to focus. At first you may find them useful just for you. As time goes on, you may decide your partner could also benefit from learning to use them. These think rules are guidelines to remember in deciding how to think about and tackle a problem.

1. Think action

Some ways of thinking about problems make you feel hopeless. Other ways of thinking about problems make you confident that you can solve them. For instance, look at the difference between these two statements:

- I'm not doing well in school. I'm too dumb to be a good student.

- I'm not doing well in school. I don't spend enough time studying, so I don't do well on exams.

When you think you can't do something because you have a certain type of personality or a certain handicap (like being "dumb"), making a change seems very difficult. When you think you can't do something because you're not taking the right actions, solutions are much more easily seen. That is the main point of the Think action rule.

When you think about problems in action terms, you not only gain hope that change can happen, but you also gain an idea of the things you need to do to make a change. From the above example, it is clear that the person needs better study skills. How she goes about getting them is another step altogether, but at least she knows there is some action she can take to make her situation better. The person who feels she is doing poorly in school because she is dumb, on the other hand, may feel like giving up. Nothing will change if she thinks she can't learn. This type of thinking leads to a giving-up attitude.

Almost any problem can be thought of in lots of different ways. If your partner is stuck in a problem and feels she has no way out, it will be useful to help her think of other ways to think about it. And when you do—Think action.

You can help your partner think action by asking her questions that get at descriptions of behavior. If she describes feeling angry and helpless about her mother's treatment of her in some situation, you can ask her exactly what happened. What was the sequence of actions by your partner and her mother that resulted in the unhappy ending?

2. Think solution

Usually, when people think about a problem, they concentrate only on the things they don't like. It can be useful, however, to think about other parts of the situation as well. When you work on solving a problem with your partner, you can help her think about it in three different ways:

1. What is wrong with the situation, or what doesn't she like about it? (Complaint)

2. How would she like things to be? (Goal)

3. How might she get to the place where she wants to be? (Action)

By helping your partner think about problems in this way, you help her see that she can have some control over her life. There are steps she can take toward finding solutions to even very difficult problems.

When you are working with the Think solution rule, encourage your partner to keep this question in mind: "What is the least I can do to change this?" Even small steps toward her goal bring her closer to it.

Here is an example of the three steps of Think solution. Toni wants to go back to school but she doesn't have anyone to look after her baby.

1. She has no child care. (Complaint)

2. She wants a baby sitter who is trustworthy, affordable, and loving towards her daughter. (Goal)

3. She can start to remedy the problem by asking people in her community for the names of baby sitters they use. She also can ask the people at WIC for the names of reputable child care agencies. (Action)

3. Think positive

Part of your job as a mentor is to help your partner build confidence in herself. The Think positive rule can help. This is a very stressful time for your partner. She may feel upset or depressed or bad about herself. Pointing out her strengths or her effectiveness in handling a situation can increase her self-confidence and self-esteem.

Positive thinking does not mean you should be unrealistically happy when unfortunate things happen. Rather, it reminds you that every situation has at least some small positive feature or consequence. Positive thinking means paying attention to good things that happen as well as bad, and not feeling that all is lost even when things look especially gloomy.

There are a few things you can do to encourage positive thinking in your partner. One is to look for things that she does well. Catch her doing something positive, and compliment her on it.

Another thing you can do is to help her set small, realistic goals that she can reach easily. It is best if her step-by-step goals start out close to what she can already do, rather than too close to her ideal standard. Positive thinking can occur naturally when she is successful at the realistic steps she has set. As she begins to feel good about herself, she will feel motivated to continue to work toward her long-term goals.

4. Think small steps

Again, small steps can be big gains in helping your partner accomplish her goals and feel good about herself. Working toward the accomplishment of small, realistic steps is easier than focusing on major, long-term goals, and makes it more likely that your partner won't give up. Big dreams and major life goals can seem overwhelming and out of reach. Although it is important to know what her long-term goals are, it is best to work toward them by a series of small steps.

Think about putting a big jigsaw puzzle together. You might think you can't do it. But if you put a few pieces together every day, and spread the task out over a period of time, you can finish the whole thing! It's the same with the things your partner wants to accomplish. She can't realize her life goals all at once, but if she works steadily on them, she can accomplish more than she thinks.

There's another important advantage to taking things in small steps instead of in great chunks. A step by step process gives your partner many chances to evaluate how things are going and decide if she wants to continue in the same direction. By seeing herself move along a planned-out path toward her goals, she will be motivated to keep moving in her chosen direction—or to revise her goals and move in a new direction.

5. Think flexible

Even the best-made plans don't always work out. Circumstances change, unexpected barriers arise, or things happen in a completely different way from what you or your partner expected. Sometimes, as your partner comes to choice points in her life, she will find doors opening where she never expected to see them. Her options may increase as she works toward the things she wants. Or she may decide, as she moves forward, that the things she once wanted are different from her current concerns. All these things are reasons to help your partner think flexibly in her planning.

You can help her to see that there are many ways to reach her goals. Even if what she is doing isn't working, all is not lost. There are usually many different things that can be done to keep her moving in the right direction—and in fact, there may be many right directions. The key is to keep an open mind.

You can use the Think flexible rule to help her learn to think creatively about her options in every difficult situation she comes across. For example, if she successfully talked her way out of a fight with her sister, you can congratulate her on how well it went, and then talk with her about what else she could have done if that strategy hadn't worked. Or, if things didn't go as she had planned, you can talk about what she could try if she is in that sort of situation again. If she talks to you about her friends, you can brainstorm with her about the things she would do if she were in a friend's situation. You can help her keep her options open, think creatively, and not give up when things don't go as she plans.

6. Think future

It is easy to get bogged down in the problems of today, especially when you are very young, pregnant, and unsure what your future will bring. Your partner may feel helpless and hopeless about being able to control her life. The Think future rule emphasizes the importance of having goals for the future, as well as taking actions today that are part of the plan for reaching future goals. If your partner doesn't think now about how she wants her life to be later, she is likely to end up where she doesn't want to be. When people don't make plans and work toward making those plans happen, they are often swept along without noticing that they are moving in a different direction than where they want to go. By making a decision to work toward something and planning how to do that, your partner will increase her chances of success.

To help your partner Think future, the two of you can talk together in depth about how she would like her life to be and the kinds of things she needs to do to make it that way. What obstacles might she run up against? What things besides those she expects to happen might happen? What would she do if her plans didn't work out? What if they did? We'll talk more about these kinds of conversations in chapter 8, when we talk about goal and value clarification.

On a smaller scale, you can help your partner Think future in her daily dealings with the world. By thinking ahead, she can anticipate many of the things she is likely to encounter during the coming week or month. She can prepare for them by talking to you and by rehearsing her future options with you. She needs to think of some of the different ways her plans could turn out, and then think flexibly—come up with different options to try depending on what happens. Whether she is planning for tomorrow or planning to meet her long-term goals, the more she plans ahead, the more likely she is to get what she wants in life.

To summarize

The think rules can help you and your partner work on making changes in her life and keeping a can-do attitude. Remember:

1. Think action.

2. Think solution.

3. Think positive.

4. Think small steps.

5. Think flexible.

6. Think future.

Happy, sad, angry, hurt, mad, depressed, blue, irritated, frustrated, afraid, overjoyed, furious—all these are feelings that everyone experiences at one time or another. Your partner may be experiencing all kinds of feelings at once about her pregnancy, about her family relationships, about the baby's father, about her future, or just about all the little hassles and tensions in her daily life.

As a mentor, much of what you will do with your partner is talking and listening. Often the most helpful way to discuss a difficult situation is to talk about feelings. You can help her deal with her feelings in two ways:

- By helping her talk things out, and

- By helping her recognize times when she needs to be more in control of her feelings

People deal with their feelings in many different ways. Your partner may be the type of person who lets everyone know what she is thinking and feeling all the time. She may tell you she's feeling upset as soon as she sees you. Or she may be a person who hides her emotions so you never know how she is feeling. Perhaps she only lets her feelings out when she is by herself, or perhaps she never seems to feel anything, even when you expect her to respond.

Probably she has more than one way of handling her emotions. It may be easy for her to show her happiness or her anger, but showing sadness may make her feel too vulnerable. On the other hand, maybe it's anger that is difficult for your partner to express. Perhaps she has learned in her family that anger means violence, so she is very afraid of her own anger.

Feelings are O.K.

Nicole's friend Dwayne was also her friend Sharon's boyfriend. When he moved away, both young women felt very sad to see him go. Nicole felt sorry for her friend, who was very upset. Even though Nicole was sad too, she felt like she had no right to feel as bad as she did because Sharon was so much closer to him. Nicole, after all, was only a friend.

Charlene's grandmother promised to take care of her son while Charlene took a night class. Unfortunately, the grandmother got sick and was unable to care for the child. Charlene felt upset and angry, but she told her friend she didn't, because she knew she couldn't blame her grandmother for being sick.

Often, people try to push aside their feelings because they think they "shouldn't feel that way" or have "no right" to a particular feeling. The fact is, however, that feelings are not right or wrong—they just are. We can't help the way we feel. So Nicole had every right to feel sad about Dwayne's leaving—even if her friend was also sad. And Charlene could feel angry and still not blame her grandmother for getting sick. Feelings are a fact of life. We can't turn them on and off like a faucet according to how we think things should be.

Though we may not be able to control what we feel, we have some control over what we do with our feelings. Some things act to intensify feelings, while others act to lessen them. It is not good to stuff feelings down inside all the time, but it is not always good to react without thinking either.

Talking it over

Sometimes, talking through a situation and the feelings involved can make your partner feel much better. Whether it's a big thing or a small one, listening to her can make a big difference in how she feels about things later. Talking things through can help in lots of different ways. It can help her:

- *Feel supported*. Your partner may simply need to be reassured that what she is feeling is okay. She may need some sympathy, or a hug, or someone to say "I would feel that way, too, if that happened to me."

- *Sort through feelings*. Your partner may have mixed feelings or be confused about things (see chapter 3). You can help her separate the different feelings from each other in order to understand herself better.

- *Figure out what's going on or what happened in a particular situation*. Talking things through can help your partner understand the situation and perhaps gain more understanding of the other people involved.

- *Think about some way to improve the situation*. As she tells you about what happened and how she feels, she may get ideas about things she could do to relieve the situation. Sometimes talking things out with the people involved may be enough.

- *Release the tension of holding feelings in*. Holding her emotions in can make your partner feel tense and upset. When she doesn't deal with feelings right away, sometimes they come out at other times, in a way that is out of proportion to the situation at hand. Instead of being mildly irritated about the baby spilling her milk, she may find herself exploding in rage. Talking things out can help keep this from happening.

- *Get another perspective on the situation*. Sometimes people are too close to the situation at hand to be able to get a clear picture of what's going on. Your partner may doubt her own perceptions and ask how the situation sounds to you. If she has low self-confidence, this may be especially important for her. She may automatically assume that the other person is right. Or she may be unable to get a clear view of her own effect on other people. You can help her see things more clearly in both kinds of situations.

Anger management

There may be times when it feels like your partner's emotions are out of control.

- She may have lost her temper and hit her child.

- She may have yelled and thrown something at the rude receptionist in her doctor's office.

- She may have made an unwise, hasty decision during a fight with her mother.

In each of these cases, your partner's anger is getting her into trouble. For times like this, she needs to learn some anger management skills.

Anger management takes three basic strategies: self-monitoring, self-evaluation, and self-appreciation.

The early warning signals of anger

The key to anger management is for your partner to notice her anger early—while it is building up—before it turns into rage.

This may mean paying attention to her body's anger signals, such as feeling heat in her face or feeling her heart pounding. It may mean thinking ahead about the possibility of getting angry before she enters a situation. Or it may

mean listening to the sound of her voice—perhaps it rises in pitch as her anger builds. These are her body's early warning signals that tell her to pay attention to what she is doing.

Interrupt the anger before it explodes

As she notices her anger mounting, she can try to interrupt it. Any number of things might work. She could leave the situation, count to 10 (or 50 or 100, if she needs to) to give herself time to calm down, call a friend, or just sit down and breathe deeply until she feels like herself again. What she does depends on the situation and on what works best for her. She may have to experiment to find out what calms her down. The most important thing for her to remember is not to act or make any important decisions while she is at the peak of her anger. If she does do something or decide something at that point, she will probably regret it later.

Check: Did it work?

It is helpful for your partner to think about how successful her attempt was after each time she practices anger control. This is the self-evaluation step. For the self-appreciation step, it may be enough to imagine the trouble she avoided by controlling her temper, or she may want to reward herself in some other way.

What to do with the anger

Although it is important for your partner to control her anger when it will get her into trouble, it is also important for her to have a chance to express this anger, once there is no danger of physically or emotionally hurting herself or someone else. This may be something she can do later with you.

Talking things through can help your partner deal with anger, but she may need active strategies as well. She may find it a relief to punch or scream into a pillow, or do some vigorous exercise to work out some of the angry energy she feels.

To summarize

- Feelings are okay. They can even be helpful!

- It helps to recognize and talk out feelings.

- Sometimes feelings must be controlled. You can put the brakes on angry feelings before they escalate out of control.

- Don't do anything or decide anything at the peak of anger.

6 Role-Playing

Role-playing can be an extremely useful tool for learning to handle difficult conversations. Role-playing is a way of practicing an event—either a situation your partner expects to encounter or a situation that she has already been in, but would like to have handled differently.

Role-playing provides an opportunity for your partner to:

- understand past events and their consequences, and

- try out different versions of future events in a safe and supportive situation.

Everybody plays roles

At first glance, role-playing may seem strange to you or your partner. When you think about it, though, we all do a little role-playing in our day to day lives. Perhaps, before you make a phone call to someone you don't know, you think through what you will say ahead of time and re-hearse it in your mind. Or perhaps you have had the experience of arguing with someone and then later going over and over the argument in your mind, thinking of all the things you wish you had said. Role-playing is very similar to these two situations, but it's a more deliberate and structured process.

When to use role-playing

There are many situations for which role-playing can be useful. Here are some examples:

- Interactions that lead to conflict or involve strong emotions—for instance, if your partner is having problems with her boyfriend, or if she thinks her mother treats her too much like a child

- Conversations about difficult topics, such as refusing to drink alcohol or getting her partner to wear a condom

- Job interviews

- Interactions with difficult people

- Important phone calls

- Interactions with helping professionals, physicians, or people at social service agencies

- Any other situation that is important or that your partner feels anxious about.

How to role-play

When people haven't role-played before, they sometimes tend to talk about what they would say in the situation, rather than simply saying it. Here's the difference:

> *You (in the role of her boyfriend):* You know I hate wearing a condom—I'm not going to do it.

> *She (NOT role-playing):* I would say that if he won't wear a condom I won't have sex with him.

> *She (role-playing):* Well that's fine, if you don't want to wear a condom. But if you won't wear one, I won't have sex with you.

By actually role-playing the situation, your partner can think about what words she would use and practice responding quickly. She has the benefit of seeing the impact her words have on someone, and of learning whether or not she is getting her point across.

Role-playing the past and the future

Role play may help your partner work through situations in the past and in the future.

In the past

By replaying a negative or confusing interaction you can help your partner practice other ways she could have handled that situation. The next time a similar situation occurs she will be prepared and able to handle it appropriately.

For example, if she is shy, she may have experiences in which she thinks she is being very forceful and yet finds people don't take her forcefulness or her anger seriously. When you role-play a past situation, you may discover that what she thinks is forceful does not come across that way at all. This is information she needs. It allows her to try out different words and tones of voice to discover what does sound as forceful or angry as she would like. Trying out and practicing some new speaking styles can enhance her confidence, as she proves to herself that she can be forceful when she wants to be.

She may be a person who often has trouble getting along with people, but doesn't understand why. Role-playing may help the two of you find some answers to that question. As in the above example, your partner may come across very differently than she thinks she does. She may feel she is acting in a perfectly civil manner, and yet people seem put off or offended by her. In role-playing a past conversation with her, you might notice something about her tone of voice, her choice of words, or her body movements that contributes to a negative conversational style she does not intend. As in the above example, sharing your reactions to her style can help her understand more about herself and make changes in those areas where she feels dissatisfied.

From these two examples, you can see how important it is to role-play rather than simply having her tell you what she would say.

In the future

There will be situations in which your partner anticipates a difficult, embarrassing, or very important interaction. Role-playing can prepare her by giving her the opportunity to plan what to say under different sorts of conditions.

For instance, role-playing could help your partner prepare for a job interview. You could act as the interviewer, asking the kind of questions you think she might encounter. She could think about how she would like to present herself and try out some answers. Even if the questions you practice with her are different from those she eventually has to answer, she will have gained an idea of the types of things she might be asked and what to expect from the situation.

After you role play

After every role play, the two of you can discuss how it went. What did each of you like about her "performance"? What did you think could be improved? It is important to compliment her on the parts of her role play you liked, in order to help her feel confident in her ability to handle situations.

Try it out another way

It is often useful to try out a few variations of the same role play. Your partner can experiment with different ways of approaching a difficult situation. You can also ask her to play her role as if she were some real or fictional person she admires. Or the two of you might switch roles. If she is really at a loss for how she might handle a situation differently, you can take her role and have her take the part of the other person involved. After seeing the strategies you use in the troublesome conversation, she can use you as a model.

To summarize

1. Role-playing can help your partner:
   - rehearse upcoming events;
   - review past events and understand their consequences.
2. After you role play together, you can:
   - discuss how it went and provide encouragement;
   - try out alternate versions of the same conversation.

Working It Out—Negotiating Skills

Tanya and her mother can't seem to agree on who should be responsible for the day-to-day care of Tanya's baby. Tanya feels that since she is his mother, she knows what's best for the baby. She feels that her mother "butts in" too much. Tanya's mother doesn't always think Tanya is doing the right things for her baby, and she believes she can do things better. Sometimes each one expects the other to be watching out for the baby but neither does, and the baby's needs go unmet.

In a situation like this, the young woman and her mother need to find a way to work things out, both so the child is well cared for and so the two of them are not always in conflict. This chapter will give you some tips about negotiation skills. These skills can be very helpful in all kinds of situations—whether it's a struggle between your partner and her mother or bargaining between you and your partner.

Negotiating styles

When there is a decision to make or a situation to work out, people have different styles of proceeding. Sometimes the hardest part of a relationship is coming to an agreement. Negotiating styles can be thought of as a continuum, with opposite extremes on either end. People may be at either end in their negotiating style, or they may be somewhere in the middle.

At one end are people who intensely dislike fighting and want to save the relationship with the other person at any cost. These people will almost always give in—even if it means giving up something they believe they deserve.

At the other end are people who always insist on having things their way. They take a position and don't budge no matter what anyone says. These people are not afraid of conflict; they seem to enjoy a good argument. The position they take in a dispute tends to get tangled up with their pride. It is almost as if a compromise would be an insult to their dignity.

When a relationship includes one person with one of these styles and one with the other:

- One person generally feels that things never go as she would like them to. She ends up resentful or feeling bad about herself.

- The solutions that are reached are usually not fair. They lead to resentment or even to the end of the relationship between them.

Such a relationship has some advantages, at least in the short run.

- One person in the relationship is a peace-keeper—making sure that the relationship is smooth and without conflict.
- One person in the relationship is willing to address points of conflict, and by addressing the conflict, creates potential for the conflict to be resolved.

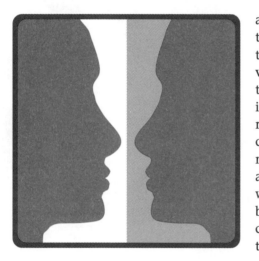

Therefore, each style has advantages and disadvantages. The important thing to realize is that for every advantage, there is a disadvantage. If either partner's style is one of these extremes, the relationship will never be completely equal. Conflicts may go unresolved if the available ways of dealing with them don't work for both people, and unresolved conflicts put strain on a relationship.

Whose side are you on?

Often, when people encounter a troublesome situation in which each person has different ideas, they feel like they're on opposite sides of the issue. Once Tanya and her mother start arguing, they may feel like they are against each other. In this case, Tanya may ask her mentor whose side she is on.

A more useful way of thinking about this situation is to think of people with different perspectives as being on the same side of the issue—but not being sure how to solve the problem. They are not working against each other; they are working together to solve the problem, even though they are working in different ways. The goal then becomes the same for both "sides"—developing a plan that is useful to everyone, rather than defeating the other point of view.

See things through her eyes

Even if it seems like the other person is doing things just to get at you, that is probably not the case. It is important to remember that she has reasons for wanting what she wants. Try to put yourself in her place and get a good sense of how she views the situation. To do this, ask her to talk about what concerns her in the situation at hand. Listen carefully, without judging or interrupting to argue. This time should be set aside for listening only. (For information on listening skills, see chapter 2.) Then switch places and present your point of view while she listens. The person talking about her own view should focus on her concerns, rather than on her version of what the outcome should be. Talk about outcomes can come later.

After both people have expressed their points of view, it may be helpful for each to sum up the concerns the other raised. This will ensure that each person is truly heard and that all concerns are explicitly recognized.

Put the concerns of both people on the table, so no one's interests are overlooked. With that information, both people can make an effort to consider the other's situation, to really see things from where the other stands. Acknowledging the validity of the other's concerns can open the door to productive compromising.

In Tanya's case, her mother explains that she doesn't see Tanya consistently acting responsibly toward her child. Sometimes Tanya is attentive and nurturing, and at other times she seems to expect her mother to care for the baby. She herself has had lots of experience with children and believes she knows what is best for Tanya's baby. Above all, Tanya's mother loves her grandchild very dearly and wants to make sure he has the best life the family can provide him.

Tanya believes she knows how to take care of her child and can understand him better than anyone else because she is his mother. At the same time, there are occasions when she simply does not know what to do with him. She doesn't like to ask her mother for advice because she thinks her mother doesn't trust her with the baby, and she doesn't want to appear incompetent. Tanya sometimes feels confused because her mother seems to alternate between taking over the care of the baby and expecting Tanya to do it all. Like her mother, Tanya loves the baby very much, and it is important to her that he have the best life she can give him.

Look for common interests

Once both people have talked about their respective interests and concerns, they can begin to see where they overlap. Tanya and her mother, for example, seem to agree on at least three things:

- Both love the baby and want to do right by him no matter what.
- Both take turns caring for the baby, but there doesn't seem to be any rhyme or reason as to who takes care of him when.
- Tanya's mother has some valuable experience and knowledge that could help her daughter. The problems come in how that knowledge should be passed down.

Define the problem together

The next step is for the two people to sit down together and decide exactly what the problem is. As discussed in chapter 4, a problem has three parts: the complaint, the goal, and the action.

1. What is the area of conflict? (Complaint)
2. How would you like things to be? (Goal)
3. What are some ideas for moving from step 1 to step 2? (Action)

Tanya and her mom come up with this set of steps:

Step 1: Complaint

- The baby needs care, but Tanya and her mother can't agree on who should be in charge of his care.

- The two women don't always agree on the best way of caring for the baby.
- Both problems lead to arguing.

Step 2: Goal

- They agree they would like to have a system that allows them to know who is responsible for the baby at any given time.
- They would both like Tanya to know more about how to take care of her baby properly.
- They would like to stop arguing so much.

Step 3: Action

- Refer to step 2 and brainstorm.

Brainstorming

After making sure each person's concerns are understood and finding some areas of common interest, it is time to come up with a variety of ideas to make the situation better. This is a time for brainstorming—thinking up as many ideas as possible, no matter how wild or crazy they may seem. This is not a time to judge ideas or throw away any that seem unreasonable. If people allow themselves to be outrageous with their ideas, not worrying about whether or not they are practical, creativity blossoms.

The purpose of brainstorming is not to find just one single solution to the problem, but to come up with a range of possibilities that the two of you can consider more seriously later.

Tanya and her mother might come up with a list that includes:

- Tanya doing all the caretaking
- Mom doing all the caretaking
- Making a schedule of care times for Tanya and Mom
- Mom offering advice any time she thinks it is needed
- Mom keeping her thoughts to herself
- Tanya taking a parenting class
- Mom helping with the baby and Tanya helping with the shopping and cleaning
- Tanya moving out of the house

Deciding which options to try

Once you have made a list of possible steps to take, you can circle the ones with the most potential. Then the different options can be discussed and agreed upon. Thinking through each option carefully can be a very important step in deciding what to do. For each potential alternative, ask:

1. Is it possible?
2. How difficult would it be to try out?
3. What do you think the consequences of this option would be?

Based on the answers to these questions, choose the option with the fewest negative consequences. Depending on how this option works out, you can expand on it, or maybe try something else.

Finding solutions that are fair

Watch out for destructive negotiating styles! It is important at this stage that the extreme negotiating styles discussed earlier don't creep in and take over. This is the time when the tendency to give in to avoid fighting, or, conversely, to stubbornly insist on your own way, can short-circuit the problem solving process. Hopefully, the processes of listening and brainstorming will lessen the impulse to work in those ways.

In some cases, agreement can occur easily. When there is still disagreement, however, it is most important that the decisions reached be fair. Decisions that are fair and useful address each person's concerns, even though people may or may not end up with what they initially hoped for. Sometimes it can be helpful to get the opinion of a third person who is not on anyone's "side." Sometimes arguments can be settled by talking to a professional, like a pediatrician, or by looking something up in a book. The fact sheets in the After the Baby Is Born section of this book provide good basic information to share with your partner.

If Tanya and her mother disagreed about when she should start feeding the baby table food, for example, they could agree to consult the child's pediatrician and act on her or his advice. This would settle their disagreement and also ensure that the baby gets good care.

To summarize

1. Think of yourselves as being on the same side, having the same goal, and working toward the best possible agreement on how to reach that goal.

2. See things through the other person's eyes.
   - Listen to the other person. Don't judge or argue.
   - Describe your concerns, but save talking about outcomes until later.
   - Tell each other what you've heard. What are the other person's major concerns?

3. Find some common interests.

4. Define the problem.
   - What's wrong?
   - How would you like things to be?
   - What are some ways to get there?

5. Brainstorm.
   - Be creative in coming up with lots of different ideas.
   - Don't judge or throw any ideas away until later.

6. Come to a fair decision.
   - Curb your tendency to give in or dig in.
   - Get a third opinion or agree on a standard ahead of time.

Moving toward Positive Change

One of the most important things you can do as a mentor is to help your partner figure out where she wants to go in her life and how to take the steps she needs to get there. With your help, she can come to understand that her life will be better if she thinks about what she wants and plans for it, rather than just letting things happen to her. You can help her do this by talking with her about her goals and values. Helping your partner clarify her goals and values will provide her with a sort of road map for her future.

Goals and values

Goals: Something to aim for

If your partner has a good mental picture of the things that are most important in her life and the situation she would ultimately like to find herself in, she will feel motivated to work toward those things. On the other hand, if she has only a vague feeling that she wants to be happy or she wants to be in a better situation, she may not be inspired to work for her goals. Goals that are too general or vague can seem overwhelming and unattainable.

The goals your partner comes up with first are not set in stone—in fact, they will probably change as other things become more important

to her. The point is that she needs something concrete to work toward. Once she has that, she can be very flexible.

Values: The seeds of goals

Your partner's values will help determine her goals. Values reflect what is most important to her, so knowing her values is a good first step in deciding on her goals. Your partner's wishes, dreams, and hopes are the seeds of her goals.

Finding her values, developing her goals

There are a number of ways you can help her find her goals and values. First of all, she may already have a good idea of how she wants her life to be. This is a good starting point for looking deeper into herself to find out what she wants in more detail.

Be creative!

Asking creative questions can help your partner discover the things that matter most to her. For instance, you could ask her how she imagines her life in ten years—or in two years.

Is she happy with that image? Is it realistic? If it is a place she would like to be, will she get there—judging from the direction she is going in now? What steps must she take in order to arrive at her ideal image?

What if the situation she imagines for herself in the future is not what she would like? What does she want instead? What must she change in her life to move toward the situation she really wants?

You could also ask her to describe a favorite family member or friend, then consider the ways that she and that person are similar and different. Focusing on ambitions, values, and priorities in life can draw attention to what is most important.

Another idea is to focus on the most important thing she has ever done. Why was this accomplishment so important to her? What values does it reflect? What did she like most about herself when she did it?

There are many questions you could ask that would clarify goals and values. Use your imagination. Discussions like these can be fun!

- Whose life would she want to imitate?

- What is her most prized possession or personal feature—and what would she trade it for?

Beware of automatic answers

When you ask questions like "What do you want to do in the future?" watch out for automatic answers. An automatic answer is a statement that answers the question, but doesn't give much real information. People develop automatic answers when they have been asked something many times, or when they have told the same story over and over. It is almost as if a button is pushed and a tape recorder spits out the answer, then rewinds until the next time the question is asked.

Automatic answers are less likely when you ask unusual or creative questions, like the ones mentioned above, but more likely when you ask questions that your partner has probably answered before. For example, to the question of "What do you want to do in the future?" your partner may answer: "I'll finish high school and then get a job" without ever thinking about what that really means.

To get beyond automatic answers, you can ask your partner to clarify or expand on what she has said. Asking for specific details can help her move beyond the general, automatic things she might say and think more clearly about what exactly her plan would involve. In the example above, it would be useful for the mentor to help her partner elaborate on her plans. Asking questions helps. For instance:

- How will she finish high school when she has a baby to care for?

- What kind of job would she like to get?

- Will she be qualified for that kind of job?

- How could she become qualified?

- How exactly will she go about getting a job?

Often, people don't think their plans all the way through. When it comes time to carry them out, they get swept along with whatever comes up and never get back to the original plan. Automatic answers may make a person feel like she knows where she's going, but in fact, they can stop her from thinking things through in detail.

Usually, people are not even aware they are using an automatic answer. They may need some help to pull themselves out of the rut. An automatic answer is like a scratch on a record. When the phonograph needle gets to the scratch, it repeats and repeats and repeats. To get on with the music, you have to give that needle a little nudge. As a mentor, you may have to give your partner a nudge to help her get on with things.

Look for common threads and themes

Once you have had some real conversations about goals and values, you can look for common themes in what your partner has said. What values or sentiments stand out from your discussions? These are the things that matter most to your partner. You can make a list of the things you see in her answers, as well as any other values she feels are very important. These values will help to determine her goals.

Five basic questions about positive change

Once you have helped your partner clarify her goals and values, she will be ready to start thinking concretely about positive changes in her life. Before she can make the commitment to take action, though, there are at least five questions that she needs to think through and answer for herself.

1. "What would life be like if I changed?"

It is important for her to think carefully about what her life would be like if she made changes. Some types of change are easy to look forward to. Other changes, such as giving up caffeine or smoking or changing her diet for the sake of her baby, may be less pleasant to imagine. Having a definite idea of some good things that will come with the sacrifices she makes can help her enjoy the prospect of changing her life-style. Help her to remember exactly why she is making these difficult changes, and to imagine what life will be like when she has made them. Encourage her to talk to you about her hopes and dreams.

2. "How will I be better off if I change?"

In order to change her life-style, your partner will have to be able to imagine how these changes will make her life better. Changing one's life-style does not automatically mean changing it for the better. To be motivated to change, your partner has to believe that the benefits resulting from the change will outweigh its disadvantages. In other words, she must be able to answer this question positively. A positive vision of the future will motivate her to change, and help her endure the drawbacks and hardships change involves. With your help, she can keep this positive vision even when she considers the drawbacks.

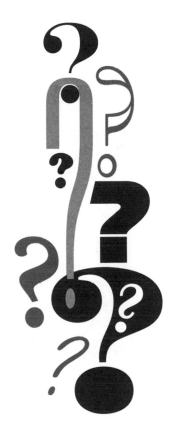

3. "Can I really make these changes?"

In addition to wondering what her life would be like and how she would be better off if she changed, your partner may also question whether she can really make the changes she needs or move in the direction she wants to go. She might not know how to proceed; she may feel she doesn't have the energy or the resources. If your partner does not believe she can accomplish what she wants to do, she may be reluctant even to try. These are important things to talk about. When you talk to her, find out about her fears as well as her hopes. Simply talking about things may help her realize that some of her fears are manageable. Encourage her to think about change in small steps, and reassure her that you will be there to help her through the tough times.

4. "What will it cost to make these changes?"

Even if your partner has a clear vision of how her life could change for the better, she may still wonder whether it will be worth all the time, energy, and effort. Encourage her to think realistically about the costs, as well as the benefits, of change. Once she has considered both the good and the bad, she will be prepared to make the change she desires. With your help, her plan of action will include ways of dealing with the hardships change involves.

5. "Can I trust my mentor to see me through?"

Although your partner may be able to answer the first four questions positively, she will still need your support and encouragement. To even be able to talk to you about her hopes and dreams and plans for the future, she has to know that she can trust you. You can help her learn to trust you by letting her know that you believe in her, and by listening to her and encouraging her to talk freely. (For more information on how to do this, please see chapters 2 and 3.)

To summarize

It is very important to help your partner formulate goals for herself. In order to decide on her goals, she must be aware of her values. You can help her discover the beliefs and opinions that are most important to her in many different ways. Open a "what if" discussion, asking her questions like:

- What if you won the lottery?
- What if you could change one thing about yourself?
- What if you could give your baby one important thing?
- What would you do?

Discussions like these can motivate your partner to think carefully about her priorities in life, and help you understand her better too. A thoughtful understanding of her values, priorities, and goals will enable her to work toward and realize her ambitions.

Beginning to Tackle a Problem

You and your partner may already have some areas in mind to work on together. However, there may be other things she needs help with that come up while you are working together. This chapter will give you some pointers on how to help her deal with problems and grow in the ways she wants to grow.

Make a list of problems

A good way to begin is to sit down with your partner and have her write a list of things she would like to work on. The items on the list can be anything from problems in school to temper outbursts to not knowing enough about babies. If there is an area that you think she would benefit from working on, you can gently bring it up. For example, she may not be aware that her diet affects her unborn baby's health. In that case, you might suggest that she write down *nutrition* on her list—meaning she needs to learn more about prenatal nutrition and needs to take care that she eats healthy food.

Sample list of things to work on

- Smoking too much
- Eating too many sweets
- Feeling down
- Controlling anger

- Learning about nutrition
- Learning about babies

Choose a problem and break it down

Once you have a list, you can ask her to tell you which things are most important or most troublesome to her. Think of problems in terms of how things are now and how she wants them to be. Remember the three parts to describing a problem:

1. What is wrong with the situation, or what doesn't she like about it? (Complaint)
2. How would she like things to be? (Goal)
3. How might she get where she wants to go? (Action)

Sample problem description— Trying not to smoke during pregnancy

Your partner was smoking before she became pregnant. Now, during her pregnancy, her physician wants her to stop smoking.

1. What is wrong with the situation, or what doesn't she like? (Complaint) She is concerned about the effects that her smoking will have on her own and her baby's health. She knows that smoking while she's pregnant is dangerous, but she is also worried about suffering from withdrawal,

as well as gaining too much weight while trying to quit smoking.

2. How would she like things to be? (Goal) She would like to develop her will power so she could stop smoking.

3. How might she get where she wants to go? (Action)

- She could talk to her health care provider to learn more about how to quit smoking.

- She could chew gum instead of smoking a cigarette when she has a craving.

- She could try to figure out when she is especially likely to crave a cigarette and devise a plan to help herself get through those times.

Identify a pattern

The next stage will help the two of you figure out how to tackle the problem. You will need to know the answers to the following three questions:

1. What usually happens *before* the troubling circumstance?

   When does it occur? Who is usually present? How does she feel beforehand?

2. What happens *during* that problematic period?

How does she think or feel during that time? What does she do? Why is this a problem?

3. What happens *after* that time?

What are the consequences of what she has done? How do other people react? How do other people's reactions make her feel? What does she do next? How does she feel afterwards?

By thinking about these three parts of the problem, you can look for patterns that may keep the problem going.

1. What happened before she smoked several cigarettes? She had been talking to her mother about her future and began to feel very nervous. Suddenly she had a craving to smoke.

2. What happened during the time she smoked the cigarettes? At first she felt less nervous, but as she continued to smoke, she began to feel guilty for smoking so many cigarettes when she should be concerned about her and her baby's health.

3. What happened afterwards? She felt very worried about seeing her doctor for a checkup. She was afraid he would tell her that she is endangering her own and her baby's health. She decided she should smoke less. However, instead of cutting down on cigarettes and substituting chew-

ing gum, she also began to eat a lot of junk food. Later, she was hungry and she felt guilty for eating all the junk food, so instead of eating something healthy, she smoked several cigarettes to cut her appetite.

Interrupt the pattern

By thinking about what she tells you, you can learn some things that might contribute to changing the pattern. In this instance the trouble started when she felt nervous and chain-smoked to calm herself. This set off a whole cycle of smoking cigarettes, indulging in irregular eating patterns, and having negative feelings about herself. Once you can see the pattern, the two of you can brainstorm together to think of ways to successfully avoid smoking or whatever she is trying to avoid. Then she can choose the best ideas and try several to see what works.

Keep long-term goals in mind

In a case such as this, your partner might become hopeless and discouraged when she slips up and reverts to her old habits. She may not see the point of trying to change her smoking habit or whatever it is she's working on. To keep her efforts strong, it is important to help her keep her goals for the future in mind. Your encouragement and belief that she can succeed will keep her hope alive. If she believes she can reach her long-term goals, she will be more likely to work toward her short-term goals. If

she achieves her short-term goals, her long-term goals are within her reach.

To summarize

1. Make a list of problems that need attention.

2. Choose one to work on and break it down into:
   - Complaint,
   - Goal, and
   - Action.

3. Make a plan to solve the problem.
   - Identify a pattern.
   - Interrupt the pattern.
   - Keep long-term goals in mind.

 Self-Management

Self-management is a problem solving strategy that can be useful in many different situations. It is especially helpful in situations that require will power or self-control, such as quitting smoking or sticking to a good diet. Self-management can also be used to help your partner avoid thinking negatively about herself or stay in control if she has a tendency to become anxious or angry.

Very simply, self-management consists of three parts: self-monitoring, self-evaluation, and self-appreciation.

Self-monitoring is noticing and paying attention to the circumstances around the thing you want to avoid doing.

Self-evaluation is keeping track of the steps you take to improve the situation and comparing yourself to a standard you set for yourself.

Self-appreciation is rewarding yourself when you do a good job with something you have been monitoring.

The self-management technique is especially helpful for several reasons.

- Your partner is in control of her actions. Although you will help her with the basic ideas and techniques, she will have a great deal of control over what she's working on. Her interest and energy for this work will be high because she is in charge of what she's doing, and she will be likely to achieve what she sets out to do.

- The technique will increase her confidence and competence. As she realizes that she can take control of different parts of her life, her sense of satisfaction will increase. She will feel like she can make changes—and she can!

- Self-management is an extremely flexible technique. Once your partner has learned it, she can take this problem solving strategy with her wherever she goes.

Your partner might experiment with the self-management technique when she is trying to understand a problem, when she is ready to work toward a new goal, or when she has a habit she would like to break.

Self-monitoring

The first part of the self-management technique, self-monitoring, is something you yourself have probably done at one time or another. Perhaps a friend mentions your habit of biting your fingernails whenever you feel impatient

about something. Maybe you've never even noticed that you do this, but from the time your friend mentions it, you begin noticing it. Now you make a conscious effort to notice when you bite your nails—or when you feel like biting your nails. Self-monitoring is a process very similar to this, but somewhat more structured. It involves paying attention to your internal cues, or feelings, then examining the situation that leads up to these feelings and how you deal with that situation.

What, when, who, why

Self-monitoring involves paying attention to the circumstances around the occurrence of the unwanted action and writing down the whats, whens, whos, and whys of the situation. The purpose is to understand what keeps the problem going strong.

To do this, you have to have a clear definition of exactly what events you are monitoring. If your partner is interested in decreasing her smoking, and is counting and recording the number of cigarettes she smokes, there is no question of what behavior she is tracking. If, on the other hand, your partner is working on decreasing the intensity of her anger, it is less clear what exactly she should be paying attention to. Should she define her anger as the irritation she feels when someone is rude to her in the supermarket? Or should she only record the instances when she gets into a raging shouting match with someone?

Look for the sequence

To help define the event your partner is tracking, ask her to notice what leads up to that event. An event like a shouting match or even lighting up a cigarette does not happen out of the blue; there is usually some sequence of events or feelings that precedes it. Before she lights a cigarette, she may have a craving that comes in combination with a craving for caffeine. This may happen every day during her break—especially on days when she's had an extremely tense morning or has felt frustrated or discouraged.

In the case of anger reduction, it is good for your partner to look for the earliest possible sign of anger that she feels. It may be that her heart starts to pound a little faster. She may notice that she is clenching her fists or her teeth.

The earlier that your partner can learn to recognize the sequence of events, the better chance she has of changing her behavior. Deciding not to smoke a cigarette when her cigarettes are still in her purse is a lot easier than deciding when one is already in her hand.

Identify a key feeling or event

It will not always be possible for your partner to know exactly how the sequence begins when she is just getting started in her self-monitoring. Initially, she may only be aware of the events that occur relatively late in the sequence. A good strategy in beginning self-monitoring is to identify one important event or feeling that usually precedes the event or feeling she is tracking.

For example, she may know that when she gets angry she feels a surge of heat in her face. She can use this as a starting point. When she feels that flush of heat, she'll know she should begin the self-monitoring process. Then she can think about what she was feeling immediately before that, as well as what she feels right at that instant. She may notice that her chest feels tight, which may cause her to recall that it has been feeling tight for some time. The next time she is in a similar situation she can pay attention to her chest muscles. If they begin to feel tight, she can read this as a warning sign that she is becoming angry.

Interrupt the sequence

The point of self-monitoring is to determine what leads up to the unwanted feeling or behavior and what keeps it going. Once the sequence of events is even partially understood, you and your partner can talk about things she could do to interrupt the sequence.

What she can do depends largely on which parts of the sequence are under her control. For instance, to return to the cigarette smoking example: the earliest step in the sequence was the fact that she had a hectic, tension-filled morning, which caused her to crave caffeine and a cigarette. It might prove difficult to change the business of the morning; however, it could be possible to change your partner's reaction to it. It is also possible to interrupt the sequence at a point that is closer to the actual smoking.

If she has a daily break with a cola or coffee and a cigarette, the whole break-time situation may stimulate her craving. Simply being accustomed to smoking at a certain time and place every day could contribute to her desire for a cigarette. If she tries to stop smoking on her break without changing any of her other habits, she will probably have a hard time quitting. But if she changes her whole break routine—by going for a walk around the block, taking her break with someone else, or having a healthy snack rather than her usual cola and cigarette—she may find it possible to quit.

Self-evaluation

The next phase of self-management is self-evaluation. Self-evaluation will help your partner note her progress toward the changes she wants to make. The information she gathers in the process can help her decide whether or not further change is needed, and what direction any further change should take.

Self-evaluation involves making a comparison between how your partner is acting or thinking or feeling and how she wants to act or think or feel. How she wants to be will be her goal or comparison standard. Her standards will be based on her previous experiences and the influences of other people and circumstances in her life. As time goes on, she can develop new standards that reflect the goals she hopes to reach. As her mentor, you can help her to adjust her old standards if they seem unrealistic or inappropriate, as well as to develop new standards for comparison.

When your partner compares her observations of herself with her internal standards, she will find herself in one of three positions:

1. She will have exceeded her standards—done even better for herself than she expected to do; or
2. She will have met her standards—done as well as she hoped to; or
3. She will have fallen short of her standards—not done as well as she hoped.

As her mentor, you can help her with her self-evaluation. Discuss her standards with her and help her compare them to her recent self-monitored performance. In discussing why she believes she did well or poorly, you can help her to arrive at an accurate and realistic reading of her performance.

Sometimes people have a hard time judging their own performance accurately. This can lead to two types of problems.

Underestimating her performance

On the one hand, your partner could underestimate how well she is doing. If her self-esteem is low, she may not be able to see the positive aspects of her performance. She may focus only on the negative when she thinks about herself, so that her self-evaluations are filled with negative remarks. This can lead her to feel even worse about herself, and less likely to see positive points next time. This negative style of thinking can lead to a vicious circle of feeling bad, thinking negatively, feeling worse, thinking more bad things, and so on, around and around.

To help your partner escape from this vicious circle, you can encourage her to focus less on major goals, where progress is difficult to see, and more on the small steps that lead up to those goals. Rather than focusing on her long-term goal (her future standard) and how far she is from it, you can help her look back to her past performance and see how far she has come. Help her focus on what she's doing now that is right, rather than on what she still does that is wrong. The last time she spoke with her mother, for instance—maybe she didn't reach her goal and future standard of completely controlling her temper, but she did restrain her urge to throw something—more than she was ever able to do in the past.

The rules of Think small steps and Think positive are very pertinent here. Every small step forward is important. The more your partner is able to focus on positives, the more her confidence will grow. If she is able to see progress in her small steps, she will become more sure of herself and more motivated to continue her effort.

Overestimating her performance

On the other hand, she may have the opposite kind of trouble in self-evaluation. She may overestimate her performance, and therefore see little need for improvement. In this case, your discussion about the comparison between her self-monitoring and her internal standards will take a different strategy. You will need to ask her questions about her perceptions very carefully, and perhaps even gently suggest some alternative explanations. If you simply tell her she is mistaken, she will probably feel defensive and disagree with you.

If, however, you discuss the situation together, and you bring up the issue gently and tactfully, she will probably feel open to hearing what you say. It is important in this case also to help her see the positive small steps she has taken. She may not have a clear idea of what she is looking for. Your assistance in pointing out small victories can help her gain an understanding of the process.

Self-appreciation

Self-appreciation is the last phase of the self-management process. Any time during the self-evaluation stage that your partner finds she has achieved small steps, encourage her to reward herself in some way. This reward could consist of a small material item, a special outing, or some other treat to remind her that she is doing a good job. You can help her think of a treat that would be especially reinforcing.

It will also help to have her tell you what steps she has taken. You can congratulate her and encourage her to take pride in her achievements. These are the stepping stones to her future! Consciously attending to her daily accomplishments, even the small ones—especially the small ones—will help her hold on to her motivation when the attainment of long-term goals seems very far in the future.

To summarize

1. The self-management technique has three parts:
   - Self-monitoring,
   - Self-evaluation, and
   - Self-appreciation.

2. Self-monitoring involves:
   - paying attention to the events that precede an unwanted behavior,
   - discovering a sequence,
   - identifying a key element in that sequence, and
   - interrupting the sequence, often by a change in routine.

Although your partner must do this for herself, a mentor can be especially helpful in the last phase, pointing out and reinforcing small steps toward the goal.

In this chapter we will walk step by step through an example of how you and your partner can work on solving a problem together.

Angie mentions to Pearl, her mentor, that she gets easily fed up with her baby not minding her. Since Pearl knows Angie has a temper, she is worried that Angie might lose control and unintentionally hurt her baby. Together they decide that it would be helpful for Angie to find some ways to deal with her anger. Let's see how Pearl and Angie work on Angie's temper.

Step 1: Identify the problem

First, Pearl helps Angie think about the problem. Once again, we break the problem into three parts:

1. What she doesn't like (the complaint),
2. How she would like things to be (the goal), and
3. How she might begin to move from here to there (the action).

What she doesn't like

Angie says she doesn't like it when:

- Her baby doesn't obey her and he's fussy.
- She gets so angry at him that she yells and shakes him.

How she would like things to be

Angie wishes:

- Her baby would mind her and wouldn't cry so much.
- She knew how to handle him better and was able to keep her cool.

How she could move from here to there

Angie thinks she could:

- Make a conscious effort to stay calm, even when he fusses.
- Learn more about why her baby fusses so much.

Pearl can help Angie realize that she needs to focus on what *she* can do—not on things over which she has little or no control. In this case, Angie can change her own behavior, but she may not be able to do anything about the baby's crying.

Pearl knows how important it is to encourage her partner, so whenever she can, she goes out of her way to be supportive of what Angie does and who she is. Pearl recognizes what an effort it was for Angie just to bring up this problem. Therefore, Pearl encourages Angie by saying something like:

"I'm proud of you because you want to work on this. I can tell how very much you care about

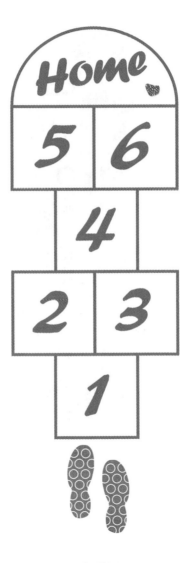

your baby and how you want to do right by him. We'll be able to work this thing through!"

Step 2: Describe the problem

The next step for Angie is to learn more about how, when, where, and why her anger occurs. In this step she will begin to pay attention to what happens around the time she feels angriest at her baby. Remember the steps of self-monitoring, from chapter 10?

Look for a clue that you are starting down the path you want to avoid.

Angie's clue, when she is becoming very angry at her son, might be clenched teeth or the feeling of heat rising in her face. She might notice one of these reactions when the baby throws his bottle on the floor for the fourth time. The key is for Angie to notice that she has started along the path to extreme anger while she is still in the early part of that sequence.

Every time this unwanted thing occurs, write down what was happening when you noticed that the sequence had started.

- What happened right before?
- What's happening right now?
- How do you feel?
- Who else is around?
- What time of day is it?

Note different aspects of the situation. Angie noted several different times that she got angry this week. One time while she was running back and forth between cooking dinner and feeding her son, the baby turned over his bowl of cereal. Another time, while she was talking on the telephone, he kept grabbing at a plant and putting the leaves in his mouth, even though she told him "No!" several times. A third time she became angry when he got into a bottle of aspirin she had left on the table and spilled it everywhere. She had just left the room for a moment to talk to her mother. After a while she noticed that each time she felt angry her face got very hot and her palms began to sweat.

Step 3: Look for a pattern

After Angie has paid attention to her anger in several different situations, she and Pearl are able to look for a pattern in her reactions. The two of them both notice that Angie seems especially likely to get angry when she is trying to do something else while she is caring for her baby.

The second pattern, which Pearl notices, is difficult for Angie to see at first. As she hears about the different episodes, Pearl begins to see that Angie really doesn't know enough about babies to understand what she can and can't expect from her son. In each of the instances that Angie told about, the baby was not being naughty; he was simply being a baby. Angie got angry partly because she thought he was purposely disobeying her. Pearl also noticed that Angie was not aware of the need to put things that might be harmful to the child out of his reach. These things together suggested to Pearl that Angie could use some help in learning about babies.

Finally, Angie's face getting hot and her palms sweating are Angie's clues that she is on the verge of becoming angry.

Step 4: Brainstorm for ideas

Now that Pearl and Angie have some idea about what is triggering Angie's anger, they can come up with things to do to make the situation better. In brainstorming, it is good to remember two rules:

1. Come up with *lots* of ideas.
2. Don't judge or throw away any ideas until there are many on the table.

These are some of the things that Pearl and Angie think Angie could try:

- When she notices her hands sweating or her face getting hot, she could leave the room.
- She could try not to do so many things at once.
- When she notices one of her anger warning signs, she could immediately try to talk herself out of being angry.
- When she notices an anger warning sign, she could ask someone to take care of her son while she goes and pounds on a pillow.
- She could get her brother or sister to hold the baby or play with him when she is busy.
- She could ask her mother some questions about babies.

- She could talk with Pearl about babies—what they need, what they can and cannot do.
- She could count to 10 before she yells or does anything.
- She could say to herself, "He doesn't do this on purpose to make me angry—he's just doing what babies do."
- She could put away things that the baby shouldn't get into.
- She could read some books about babies.

Step 5: Decide which things to try

The next step is deciding which ideas are likely to be the best for Angie. These questions are helpful for choosing solutions:

1. What is possible to do—and what is easiest to do?
2. What are the long- and short-term consequences of the different options?
3. What would need to be done in order to try out an option?
4. What would I like to do?

After talking things through, Angie and Pearl decide that Angie needs to do three things. First, she needs to learn something about what she can and cannot expect from her son as he moves through different stages. That way she will understand him better and be less likely to get angry at him. She could learn about babies by talking to people like her mother and Pearl, or she could do some reading. Looking back at the four questions above, they decide that:

- Either of these last options is possible.

- One possible consequence of talking to her mom is that her mother may appreciate Angie's asking her and they may grow closer—or she may begin to feel overly responsible for the child, which she has already said she doesn't want.

- For Angie to talk to her mother or Pearl, she need only begin to ask questions. To read, she needs to get a book. Neither option poses too many problems.

- Angie might like to talk about things when she's feeling talkative, and read when she feels like being alone. She can imagine liking either option.

They decide that in this case, all three options are practical and so she will do a little of each. Angie and Pearl decide to spend some of each of their times together talking about babies.

The second solution is to try not to do lots of different things at once. This seems to be overwhelming to Angie, so she is likely to become irritated. To avoid doing lots of things at once, she decides (after looking over her options and thinking about the four questions) to ask her brothers and sisters to help her out a little more.

The third thing Angie needs to do is to pay attention to her anger warning signals and work towards nipping her anger in the bud, before it gets out of hand. This is a good time to use the self-management process described in chapter 10. After she decides which strategies from her list to use (counting to 10, talking herself out of being angry, pounding a pillow—all instead of taking out her anger on her son) she can start the self-management process.

Step 6: Put the self-management plan into action

Once again, the steps are:
- self-monitoring,
- self-evaluation, and
- self-appreciation.

Angie plans to do the following:

1. Watch for her anger warning signals. When she notices herself becoming angry she will use one of the strategies.

2. After the anger has passed, she will think about how well she handled the situation, comparing it to how well she has handled things in the past.

3. When she does well, she will reward herself with a new bottle of nail polish or some time in the park with her son.

To summarize

1. Identify the problem.
   - What she doesn't like
   - How she would like things to be

- What she might do to begin to move from 1 to 2

2. Describe the problem.
   - Look for a clue that she is starting to travel toward the thing she wants to avoid.
   - Write down what is happening when she notices the sequence has started.

3. Look for a pattern.

4. Brainstorm for ideas.
   - Come up with *lots* of ideas.
   - Don't throw out any ideas right away.

5. Decide which things to try.
   - What is possible to do?
   - What are the long- and short-term consequences of the different options?
   - What would it take to try out each option?

6. Put the self-management plan into action.
   - Self-monitoring
   - Self-evaluation
   - Self-appreciation

Being a mentor will not always be easy. There may be times when you feel discouraged and want to give up. Your partner may miss meetings with you, ignore your advice, do things that are not in her best interests, or even show hostility. Mentoring can be emotionally intense! It is important to take care of yourself so you don't become overloaded or "burned out."

Burnout can happen if you put everything you've got into your relationship with your partner and she doesn't respond the way you expect. It may cause you to feel fed up, discouraged, hopeless, and angry. At first, your inclination may be to put even more time and energy into the relationship to try to make it better. Unfortunately, this may make things worse if she fails to respond as you hope. You may begin to feel like your partner will never amount to anything. You may just want to quit.

When you're feeling burned out, it's hard to be helpful to your partner, and it's hard on you as well. The good news is that there are ways to prevent burnout. All the strategies to avoid burnout focus on ways for *you* to think about and deal with being a mentor. You can't change the way your partner acts, but you can change how you think about what is happening between the two of you. This chapter deals with things to do to prevent burnout.

Keep your expectations reasonable

You are full of good ideas and suggestions to help your partner get on the right path. You can imagine lots of positive changes she could make. You have big dreams for her.

Unfortunately, big dreams don't always come to pass as smoothly and easily as we might hope. Although developing goals with your partner is a crucial step in helping her improve her life, it is important to strike a balance between hope and reality in what you expect of her. There are many things your partner can do to improve her life situation. There are also some things she may not be able to do. If you keep realistic goals in mind, you will not be disappointed (and face burnout) because your big dreams for her don't work out the way you hoped.

It might help to remember the Think small steps rule from chapter 4. Instead of judging her progress by the big goals you have in mind for her,

think small steps—that is, focus on the small advances she has made. Maybe she hasn't yet enrolled in the training program the two of you have been talking about, but at least she is thinking about it—whereas before, she didn't have any clue about what she wanted to do after high school. This is progress!

Keep in mind that change is hard work. It never comes easily. You may see your partner backslide in her progress, even when you think she is doing well. Don't let this discourage you. It's completely normal. Chances are she will be back on track soon.

Half empty or half full?

When you look at a glass of water, you might see it as half empty or you might see it as half full. It all depends on your perspective. The same is true about your partner's situation. You can focus on the positive aspects, or you can focus on the negative. The way you look at the situation can make a big difference in how you feel about it. Sometimes the negatives seem overwhelming—so much so that you forget to look forthe positive.

Focusing on the bad parts of a situation can lead to burnout. To avoid falling into the burn-out trap, remember the Think positive rule. Finding the positive aspects of a situation can help both you and your partner avoid discouragement. This is not to say that every cloud has a silver lining—many clouds seem to be gray all the way through. But there are often bits of goodness to be found even in bad situations. When the cloud is especially gray, perhaps the best approach is to Think future—remembering that every new day brings new possibilities.

You are accomplishing more than you think

You may expect that the time you spend with your partner will lead to large, noticeable changes in her life. This may or may not be the case. If it is not, don't be discouraged. You are probably having a bigger effect than you can see.

Just listening to your partner is more helpful than you might think. Sometimes you may wish you had lots of good advice to give her, but just listening—really listening—is *very* important. You may be the only person she knows who will truly pay attention to her. Simply hearing and understanding what she says is very supportive.

Discussing things with her is also more helpful than you may sometimes think. Even if she doesn't seem to be paying attention, chances are she will remember some of what you say and tuck it away in her mind. Later, you may hear her say the same thing you said—and think it is her own idea! Don't underestimate the power of your words.

Don't give up on her

Your partner may act like she's not interested in your ideas, making you feel hurt and discouraged. But don't give up on her! Maybe she's had bad experiences with people she trusted in the past, so she's wary of trusting anyone. Be patient. Let her know you are there and you intend to stay around in case she needs you. Sticking around when she expects you to give up sends the very powerful message that she is worth something and that you care enough about her not to run.

You send another powerful message when you take every opportunity to express your confidence in her and to tell her that you like something she has done. These messages will all sink in somehow, building her self-esteem and self-confidence. Even when she does something you don't like, you still like her—and you can tell her so. You can even use those very words: "I don't like what you did, but I still like you."

Again, this sends the message that you are willing to stick by her, while at the same time letting her know that whatever she did was not acceptable. This message will be stronger still if you can find something to like or praise her for even when she does things you don't like. Maybe you can remind her of something she did in the past that you really liked, or maybe you can praise her intentions while letting her know that she went about something the wrong way.

The point is that even in those times when you think you're not getting through to her, when you think she hasn't even heard what you said, chances are that more got through to her than you think. Even if she doesn't show it at the time, you are helping her.

She is responsible for herself

To protect yourself from burnout, it is important to remember that you are not responsible for your partner. She has to be responsible for herself. You can help her, you can support her, you can give her little pushes in the right direction—but you can't do things for her. Only she can make changes in her life.

Setting limits

This may mean setting some limits with her early in the relationship. She may expect you to do everything for her—lending her money, driving her around, baby-sitting—and you might be tempted to do just that. Doing too much for her, however, will not help either of you in the long run. She will become overly dependent on you and she will not learn to do things for herself. You may get tired, resentful, and burned out. A better strategy is to support and encourage her while she does things on her own. She'll appreciate your support, and she'll learn to do the things she needs to do.

Other mentors can help

Talking to other mentors can be a great comfort. They may have gone through experiences very like what you and your partner are going through now. Another mentor may be able to suggest something that was helpful to her in a similar situation, or she may just be a friendly listener who understands what being a mentor is all about.

When you are under pressure

Mentors may be especially prone to burnout when they are under pressure in other parts of their lives. If you are having personal problems with your family or an especially difficult time at work, you may need to ease up on your commitments and take a short break. People who help others (like mentors) can easily feel overwhelmed by the problems they face.

If you are feeling worn out—either physically or emotionally—you may need to take a break from your partner and get some support for yourself. This might mean rescheduling your meeting time to another day or having a short phone conversation with her rather than your usual evening together. You can explain to her that you're worn out and need a break, but you're looking forward to seeing her the next time. If you see her while you are feeling too rundown, chances are neither of you will gain much from it.

Perhaps the best strategy is to take some time for yourself before you get to the point of needing to reschedule time with your partner. If you are feeling under pressure in your life in general, that's a sign you need to give yourself a little care. Maybe you need to schedule a walk in the park sometime during the day, or an hour of reading, or a long bath. Maybe you need to find someone you can talk to about whatever is on your mind. A little time off every day can do you a world of good—and make you less likely to burn out.

Just caring is important

The main thing to remember is that even though you may not always feel like you're doing all you can for your partner, you care about her. And that alone is worth a great deal. Being a mentor is a priceless gift you have chosen to give to your young partner and her baby. Your relationship will not only make a big difference in her life, but it may also make a big difference in her baby's life. It takes a very special person to make a commitment to a young woman the way you have. You should feel proud.

Fact Sheets

♦ ♦ ♦ ♦ ♦ ♦ ♦ ♦ ♦ ♦ ♦

I WHAT EVERY PREGNANT WOMAN SHOULD KNOW

II AFTER THE BABY IS BORN

III HIV AND AIDS: ESSENTIAL INFORMATION

The Fact Sheets section of the manual is designed to provide you with information and facts that are relevant to your partner and her baby. There are two purposes for providing you with this information. First, the fact sheets can be useful for helping you gain a greater understanding of the factors affecting your partner as a pregnant and parenting teenager. Second, throughout the course of your relationship with your partner, you will find that your partner has many questions and concerns about her pregnancy, and about being a parent.

These fact sheets cannot take the place of your partner asking her doctor or health care provider for information, but they can serve as another helpful source of information. Hopefully, the information provided in this section will help you to answer some of your partner's questions. Beyond being supportive to your partner, you will be a source of necessary information that will help her and her baby be healthy.

Sources and Resources, the reading list at the end of this section, includes the materials used in the preparation of these fact sheets plus other materials you and your partner may find helpful.

Eating Well during Pregnancy

Many teenage mothers have low-birthweight babies because they do not gain as much weight as they should. These babies often have trouble staying healthy, and may even die.

It is extremely important for women to eat well during pregnancy. People used to think that the nutrients in the food the mother ate went to the baby first, and then to the mother. We now know that the reverse is true. The food eaten by a pregnant woman nourishes her body first, and only supplies her child with what is left over. If there is not enough to go around, the baby does not get the food it needs to grow strong and healthy. That's why it is crucial for pregnant women to eat enough good food—to make sure enough is left over to nourish the baby.

Eating well is *especially* important for teenage mothers, who haven't finished with their own growing yet. They need even more good, nutritious food than pregnant adults. Pregnant teenagers who haven't finished growing are particularly likely to have low-birthweight babies or medical complications. Encourage your partner to choose her foods very carefully. Judith E. Brown, in *Nutrition for Your Pregnancy,* suggests the following daily diet for pregnant teenagers:

- **Dairy products—5 servings**
  (milk, yogurt, cheese, cottage cheese)

- **Meat and meat alternatives—3 servings**
  (fish, poultry, dried beans like kidney beans and lentils, eggs, peanut butter)
- **Vitamin A vegetables—1 serving**
  (yellow and orange vegetables like carrots and sweet potatoes, greens like collards, turnip and beet greens, spinach and broccoli)
- **Vitamin C fruits and vegetables— 2 servings** (oranges, orange juice, grapefruit, tomatoes, peppers, broccoli, strawberries)
- **Other fruits and vegetables—1 serving**
  (bananas, corn, green beans, apples)
- **Breads and cereals—5 servings**
  (bread, muffins, cereal, pasta, rice)

Your partner's diet should also include at least **10 cups of water and other fluids** each day.

Fluid Intake during Pregnancy ◆ ◆ ◆ ◆ ◆ ◆ ◆ ◆ ◆ ◆ ◆ ◆

Women often want to know whether they should drink more fluids during pregnancy. The answer is *YES!* There are several reasons why increased fluid intake is necessary during pregnancy.

Drink fluids to feel good

Many women suffer headaches, swelling, and other problems during pregnancy. Some of these problems get better when the pregnant woman drinks more water than she normally does.

Pregnant women need extra fluids

One of the major changes that occurs to a woman's body during pregnancy is an increase in blood volume. A pregnant woman's body starts producing more blood to satisfy the needs of the growing fetus. Blood volume may increase 50 percent or more. To keep up with this change, the body needs extra liquids.

Avoid hemorrhoids and constipation

Hemorrhoids and constipation are common problems during and after pregnancy. Sometimes hemorrhoids are caused by constipation. The best treatment is to avoid constipation in the first place. One way to do that is to increase your intake of liquids and fiber. The body needs both of these for all of its systems, including the digestive system, to function properly.

What kind of fluids should a pregnant woman drink?

The best fluid for the body is water. However, some women enjoy drinking water with a little fruit juice added for flavor. This is healthy and tasty, as well as refreshing. Many pregnant women find it helpful to have a glass of water or milk nearby all through the day.

What kind of fluids should a pregnant woman avoid?

Avoid fluids that contain a lot of calories, artificial sweeteners, or chemicals, such as caffeine. Sodas should generally be avoided, as should coffee, and of course, alcohol. A general rule during pregnancy is to avoid eating or drinking anything that has little or no nutritional value.

Gaining Enough Weight ◆ ◆ ◆ ◆ ◆ ◆ ◆ ◆ ◆ ◆ ◆ ◆ ◆ ◆ ◆

Besides eating well, it is important for your partner to gain enough weight. While there is no hard and fast rule about how much weight to gain during pregnancy, there are some guidelines. In general, women who were underweight before their pregnancy began should gain relatively more weight than women who were overweight before their pregnancy. Your partner should talk to her health care provider about how much weight to gain.

The weight the mother gains while she is pregnant determines in part how much her baby will weigh when it is born. Babies who are born weighing between 7 pounds, 14 ounces and 9 pounds are the healthiest, while those weighing less are at greater risk of illness and death. The average weight of babies born in the United States is only 7 pounds, 6 ounces—and teenagers often have babies weighing even less. Babies who weigh 5 pounds, 8 ounces or less at birth are considered low-birthweight babies, and often have many problems because of their small size.

Low-birthweight babies are more likely to get sick than heavier babies. They can also be less intelligent. They may be hyperactive. They may even die.

The chances of delivering a low-birthweight baby are highest for teenagers, women who were underweight before pregnancy, and women who are undernourished. Teenagers who eat a nutritious diet and receive regular prenatal care reduce their chances of giving birth to low-birthweight babies.

Snacks

Teenage girls are often not very careful about what they eat. Most teens eat much of their food between meals. Snacks are OK—as long as they are healthy rather than "junk food."

Some healthy snacks are:

- peanut butter and crackers,
- fruit,
- raisins, and
- yogurt.

Dieting

Many girls are concerned about their figures and already have experience with dieting. It is critically important for your partner to understand that now is not the right time to diet or cut back on eating. Her baby needs nourishing food so it can be healthy and strong when it is born.

Eating to Prevent Problems ◆ ◆ ◆ ◆ ◆ ◆ ◆ ◆ ◆ ◆ ◆ ◆ ◆

Even if she is overweight when she becomes pregnant, pregnancy is not the time to diet! During the early stages of pregnancy, the young mother-to-be may not want to eat much because she feels sick. Late in the pregnancy she may not be able to eat much because the baby takes up so much room. Even though it may be hard for the mom-to-be to eat, *it is important that she continue to eat well!* Certain foods and eating patterns can relieve some of the common problems associated with pregnancy.

Morning sickness and nausea

Here are some suggestions to help your partner lessen morning sickness or nausea during the day.

- She can try getting up slowly rather than jumping out of bed. Sitting up for a few minutes first can help her to feel less sick.

- She can eat dry toast or crackers before getting out of bed.

- She can eat smaller meals throughout the day rather than having three large meals. Nausea is sometimes more intense with an empty stomach.

- She can drink liquids between meals rather than with meals.

- She can try eating starchy foods like bread and pasta and avoid eating or smelling foods that make her feel nauseous. Certain tastes and smells, such as coffee, beer, and fried foods, can bring on or intensify nausea in some women.

- She can eat foods that are rich in vitamin B6. Some foods rich in vitamin B6 are turnip greens, Brussels sprouts, kidney beans, bananas, chicken, black-eyed peas, and potatoes.

Heartburn

Heartburn is another problem that many women experience, especially during late pregnancy. Heartburn is caused by the pressure of the baby on the stomach. This pressure can cause digestive juices from the stomach to shoot up into the esophagus and cause pain near the heart.

Heartburn is more likely when the stomach is very full, so eating small meals frequently helps prevent it. Your partner may find that her heartburn is eliminated by avoiding certain foods, such as spicy dishes, fried or fatty foods, and processed meats.

Constipation

Another common problem in pregnancy that can be alleviated through diet is constipation. Constipation is often caused by the hormone progesterone, which is released in high doses during pregnancy. Progesterone decreases the strength of the muscles in the intestines—which makes the passage of food through them slower and more difficult. As the unborn baby grows bigger, its weight on the mother's intestines may add to constipation problems. If constipation is not taken care of, it may lead to painful hemorrhoids.

There are at least three things that can help prevent or clear up constipation:

- Drinking lots of fluids (at least 10 servings per day)
- Exercising
- Eating a high fiber diet

Fiber is found in many foods, especially in whole grains and fresh fruits and vegetables. It helps digestion because it absorbs water and makes stools softer and easier to pass through the intestines. Your partner needs dietary fiber every day. Here are some foods that are rich in fiber.

- Bran cereals
- Rolled oats
- Red beans, kidney beans, peas, and other legumes
- Carrots
- Shredded wheat
- Whole wheat bread
- Bran muffins
- Cabbage
- Green salads
- Fresh fruit

Prenatal Vitamins & Over-the-Counter Medications

Doctors often prescribe prenatal vitamins for a pregnant woman. They are the most important supplement to take during pregnancy. Prenatal vitamins are different from regular vitamins because they contain higher levels of iron and folate, which women need at this time.

Prenatal vitamins are not a substitute for food. Instead, they are a necessary supplement to a healthy pregnancy diet. Vitamins are also often prescribed for the woman who chooses to breastfeed.

Sometimes prenatal vitamins are difficult to tolerate. They can be irritating to the stomach or cause constipation. To reduce irritation, the pregnant woman should take the vitamins with meals, or at night before bed.

Iron Supplements

Some doctors also prescribe iron supplements for pregnant women. Sometimes the supplements are taken in addition to the prenatal vitamins (which contain iron); sometimes they are prescribed without the vitamins. Iron is the most important single supplement during pregnancy.

Sometimes women have side effects from taking iron supplements. These include nausea, stomach irritation, and constipation. Perhaps these side effects can be reduced by decreasing the amount of iron taken in supplement form.

To get more iron in natural form, foods such as liver and spinach can be added to the diet. However, the pregnant woman should always talk to her doctor before reducing the amount of iron she is taking.

Medications

Pregnant women should not take any medicines during pregnancy without first asking their health care provider. This goes for prescription drugs such as antibiotics and also for over-the-counter drugs such as aspirin, laxatives, nose drops, cold medicines, cough syrups, and antacids. Many people do not consider over-the-counter treatments as medications, and do not worry about the safety of these products. However, many over-the-counter medications may not be safe during pregnancy.

If your partner takes a prescription medication regularly for some condition, such as high blood pressure, she should inform her doctor as soon as she suspects she is pregnant. Her doctor will be able to advise her about whether she needs to discontinue her medication, and if so, how to do it safely.

Common medications to avoid during pregnancy

- Cough syrups and sleep medications that contain alcohol. Taking these

during pregnancy is as dangerous as
drinking wine or beer.

- Aspirin
- Ibuprofen (found in Advil™ and
  Motrin™)
- Antacids containing sodium bicar-
  bonate or aluminum
- Accutane™ (commonly prescribed
  for treatment of acne)

A pregnant woman should consult a doctor
before using any medication.

Other Things to Avoid during Pregnancy ◆ ◆ ◆ ◆ ◆ ◆ ◆ ◆ ◆ ◆

Cat Litter Boxes

If she lives with a cat, your partner should have someone else empty the litter box. Contact with cat feces can cause toxoplasmosis in the mother-to-be. Toxoplasmosis occurs from accidental ingestion after coming in contact with the feces of an infected cat. In people who are not pregnant, toxoplasmosis can feel like a case of the flu. For the unborn baby, the effects are much more serious. Toxoplasmosis can result in blindness, mental retardation, and other birth defects. Pregnant women should always wash their hands after handling cats.

Raw meat

Raw meat may cause similar problems. Meat that a pregnant woman eats must be cooked thoroughly, and she must wash her hands after handling raw meat.

Drugs

Both street drugs and legal drugs can have very serious effects on the growing fetus. These include illegal drugs such as marijuana and cocaine, prescription drugs, some medicines that can be bought without a prescription, and caffeine. Before your partner takes any drugs or medicines, she should talk to her health care provider. For more information please see the fact sheet on Drugs and Pregnancy.

Vitamins or supplements

Your partner should talk to her health care provider before using any vitamins or supplements other than the ones specifically prescribed for her to use at this time. Some vitamins can build up in the body and become toxic.

Workplace hazards

Your partner should be careful to avoid exposure to chemicals or radiation. Because she may come in contact with hazardous substances at her job, she should check with her employer to find out what dangers are present in the workplace. For example, factories often use industrial chemicals, and people in hospitals may work near x-ray machines. Exposure to certain toxic chemicals has produced miscarriages and babies with low birthweight or birth defects. Here are some hazards to avoid:

- anesthetic gases
- industrial solvents
- lead
- pesticides
- radiation

Alcohol, cigarettes, and drugs

Smoking, drinking, and drug use can cause serious problems for the baby. For more information, please see the fact sheets on these topics.

Artificial sweeteners

Saccharin (sold under the name Sweet 'n Low™) is not safe for use during pregnancy. Pregnant women should avoid this product. Aspartame (sold under the brand names Nutrasweet™ and Equal™) has not been found harmful to healthy pregnant women. However, as a rule, it is wise to avoid using any kind of artificial sweetener during pregnancy. Diet sodas and other products containing artificial sweeteners generally contain numerous artificial ingredients, and have little nutritional value. To grow a strong, healthy baby, a pregnant woman needs to choose foods that are rich in nutrition, and should avoid artificially sweetened foods and beverages.

Douching

Many women wonder whether or not they should douche while they are pregnant. Generally, doctors recommend that pregnant women avoid douching. Many women are tempted to douche when they suffer a yeast infection or other irritation. However, during douching, water is flushed up into the vagina, and can actually push the infection higher into the woman's body. The end result can be a worse infection that becomes a risk to the fetus.

What about sex?

This question may never come up with your partner. Then again, it might. Misinformation and folklore abound on this topic. Most doctors today agree that if the pregnancy is progressing normally, sex is safe as long as it's comfortable.

Exercise during Pregnancy ◆ ◆ ◆ ◆ ◆ ◆ ◆ ◆ ◆ ◆ ◆ ◆ ◆ ◆

It's a good idea for women to speak to their doctors before initiating a new exercise program during pregnancy. This is especially true for anyone who has had a previous miscarriage or premature delivery.

During pregnancy, the whole body goes through enormous changes. Pregnancy and childbirth are a time to be as strong and healthy as possible. Exercising in pregnancy can help in some aspects of childbirth, but not in others. For instance, exercise won't help the cervix dilate any better, and it won't speed up labor. Nevertheless, moderate exercise is something good your partner can do for herself. There are several ways that exercising can be beneficial. Moderate, regular exercise:

- Builds the body's strength and energy for the months ahead;

- Tones up and strengthens muscles, which can increase the ease of delivery;

- Can lessen some of the aches that come from being pregnant, such as lower back pain;

- Helps reduce stress; and

- Makes it easier to get back in shape after the pregnancy.

Body changes during pregnancy

The body goes through many changes during pregnancy. Some of these are less obvious than others. Knowledge of these changes is necessary in order to avoid injuries or problems for both mother and baby.

One of the more obvious changes is that the mother's abdomen gets bigger and her center of gravity shifts, thus making her prone to lose her balance and fall. A less obvious change is that knee, ankle, and wrist joints become more susceptible to injury because pregnancy hormones change the connective tissue around the joints. Pregnancy also makes the body's temperature rise more quickly, so the mother can easily become dehydrated. Overheating can also harm the fetus.

Tips for beginning to exercise

Because of all these changes in the body, it is important to begin exercising slowly and gradually. If your partner hadn't been exercising at all before her pregnancy, this is not the time to begin a strenuous new sport. In fact, sometimes women feel too sick or rundown in the first trimester to begin exercising. If that is the case, it may be better for her to wait until the second trimester, when she is likely to feel better, to start an exercise program.

Exercises well-suited to pregnancy

- walking
- stretching
- swimming
- low-impact aerobics

During exercise, your partner should

- wear layers that she can take off while she is exercising. This will help her remain comfortable and avoid overheating.
- wear good support shoes.
- drink lots of fluids to avoid dehydration.
- avoid exercising on an empty stomach.

Some cautions

There are certain things to be extra careful about while exercising during pregnancy.

- Your partner should be careful to slow down when she becomes tired.
- She should avoid becoming overheated.
- She should be sure that her heart rate does not get too high. She can check her heartbeat immediately after exercising by taking her pulse at the wrist or on her neck near her jaw. If she counts her pulse rate for 10 seconds, and multiplies this number by 6, she will have the number of beats per minute. For most women, it is best to keep the heartbeat under 140 beats per minute.

- After the fourth month of her pregnancy, your partner should avoid exercising on her back or her stomach.

Knowing when to stop

If she exercises during pregnancy, is very important for your partner to know when to stop. The most important thing is for her to listen to her body. In general, if her body doesn't feel good, she should stop.

Specific reasons to stop include:

- pain,
- vaginal bleeding,
- extreme shortness of breath or dizziness, and
- becoming too tired.

If your partner has any questions or concerns about exercising, encourage her to ask her health care provider.

Sleep Positions during Pregnancy

Many pregnant women have questions about their sleeping positions and habits and how these affect the developing fetus.

Sleeping on her back

Although finding comfortable sleeping positions gets more difficult as the pregnancy progresses, it is best if the pregnant woman does not sleep on her back. As the woman's uterus gets larger and heavier during pregnancy, sleeping on her back can place the uterus on top of important blood vessels that run down the back of her abdomen. This pressure on the blood vessels can decrease circulation to the fetus and to parts of the woman's body. Also, some pregnant women may find it harder to breathe when they sleep on their backs.

Sleeping on her stomach

A pregnant woman should also avoid sleeping on her stomach. This puts pressure on the developing fetus, especially when the woman's uterus starts getting very large. As the pregnancy progresses, it will also become very difficult and uncomfortable for the woman to sleep on her stomach.

Finding comfortable ways to sleep

It is easiest for the pregnant woman if she starts learning to sleep on her side early in the pregnancy. Then, as the pregnancy develops, she will already be used to this sleeping position and she will lose less sleep trying to get comfortable. Many women find it useful to add a few extra pillows for support. For example, the pregnant woman may want to put a pillow behind her so if she rolls on her back, she won't be lying flat. She may also want to put a pillow between her legs when she's lying on her side.

Smoking and Pregnancy ◆ ◆ ◆ ◆ ◆ ◆ ◆ ◆ ◆ ◆ ◆ ◆ ◆ ◆ ◆ ◆

Smoking is hazardous to your health—and to the unborn baby's health!

Problems smoking can cause

Smoking during pregnancy has been associated with a number of very serious problems. Women who smoke are especially likely to have low-birthweight babies, who are at greater risk than other babies of dying soon after birth. Pregnant women who smoke also have high rates of miscarriages, stillborn babies, and premature deliveries. Crib death, or Sudden Infant Death Syndrome, is also associated with smoking during pregnancy.

The more cigarettes a woman smokes during her pregnancy, the greater her risk of having a low-birthweight baby. The fewer cigarettes she smokes, the better are her chances of delivering a healthy baby. Therefore, cutting down can make a difference. In fact, if a woman quits smoking by her fourth month of pregnancy, her chances of delivering a low-birthweight baby are similar to those of a nonsmoker.

Why smoking is harmful to the baby

The developing fetus needs oxygen-rich blood delivered through the placenta. When the mother smokes, her blood vessels tighten and less oxygen is able to reach the baby. Smoking may also lower the amount of nutrients that reach the baby. Changing to low-tar cigarettes does *not* alleviate smoking-related problems in pregnancy.

After the baby is born

Smoking is also bad for nursing mothers. Nicotine slows down the production of breast milk and reduces its vitamin C content. When a nursing mother smokes, the nicotine from her cigarettes is found in her breast milk. If the baby drinks breast milk containing nicotine it takes the nicotine into its body. This is very unhealthy for the baby. Babies raised in homes where people smoke also have more breathing problems than other babies. It's best for the mother and the baby if the mother doesn't smoke.

Alcohol and Pregnancy ◆ ◆ ◆ ◆ ◆ ◆ ◆ ◆ ◆ ◆ ◆ ◆ ◆ ◆ ◆

One question that pregnant women often ask is "Can I drink alcohol during my pregnancy?" The answer is *NO!*

When a woman drinks beer, wine, wine coolers, or hard liquor while pregnant, she is putting herself and her child at risk for a variety of problems. A woman who has three or four drinks a day greatly increases her risk for vaginal bleeding, spontaneous abortion, and premature delivery. Fetal alcohol syndrome (FAS) and fetal alcohol effects (FAE) are the terms for problems suffered by babies whose mothers drink alcohol during pregnancy.

What are FAS and FAE?

Fetal alcohol syndrome is the name for the complete set of problems associated with a woman's drinking during pregnancy. Fetal alcohol effects refers to the individual problems. Drinking during pregnancy increases the risk that a baby will be born with some or all of these problems. Babies with FAS or FAE may have the following problems:

- Low birthweight and a slow rate of physical development
- Mental retardation. Drinking by pregnant mothers is the third leading cause of mental retardation in U.S. children today.

- Malformed head, face, and limbs. FAS and FAE babies can have smaller than normal heads, narrow eyes with droopy lids, flattened faces and upper lips, cleft palates, and muscular and skeletal problems.
- Hyperactivity or restlessness, sleep disturbances in early infancy, short attention span, and delays in psychological development
- Heart or kidney problems
- Poor sucking response
- Poor coordination
- Learning disabilities and various behavioral problems

Drinking at *any time* during pregnancy can cause harm. Drinking alcohol during the first trimester is especially harmful, because this is when the baby's organs are forming. But even if your partner drank before she knew she was pregnant or early in her pregnancy, there is every reason for her to stop now. She will be healthier, and she will feel more like eating, exercising, and following through on other suggestions you and her doctor give her. Stopping drinking at *any point* increases the chances of having a healthy baby.

The good news is that FAS and FAE can be prevented. When the mother avoids drinking alcohol during her pregnancy, her baby will not suffer from FAS or FAE. Because no one knows if there is any safe level of alcohol consumption during pregnancy, the American Medical Association, the March of Dimes Birth Defects Foundation, and the Surgeon General all advise abstinence as the only safe course.

Strategies to avoid drinking

Sometimes not drinking for the whole pregnancy can seem like a sacrifice to a woman for whom alcohol is a regular part of life. Here are some strategies to help your partner avoid drinking during her pregnancy:

- She can avoid situations in which she might be tempted to drink, and places where alcohol is served.

- She can lessen peer pressure to drink by explaining to others that she does not want to harm her baby.

- She can decide not to drink just for today. Making the decision not to drink just for one day can be easier than deciding to abstain for nine months.

- She can take pride in the fact that she is giving up drinking for the sake of her baby. She is giving her baby a precious gift, and she should be proud of herself!

- She can talk to you or someone else to help her figure out other strategies.

Alcohol use by pregnant women is the third leading cause of birth defects and mental retardation. Of all the major causes of birth defects, FAS and FAE are the only ones that can be prevented.

Drugs and Pregnancy

Other drugs besides tobacco and alcohol are very dangerous to a pregnant woman and her developing baby. The pregnant woman who uses illegal drugs increases her risk for miscarriage, premature birth, stillbirth, and infant death.

She also increases her risk of delivering a low-birthweight baby. Low-birthweight babies may have a harder time surviving than other babies because their bodies and some of their systems are not fully developed. They are likely to suffer from a variety of physical and mental challenges that can affect them for their entire lives.

Everything a woman does while she is pregnant affects both her life and that of her baby. Women who use drugs while they are pregnant risk hurting their babies' chances for a healthy life. Learning the facts about drugs and pregnancy is an important first step in protecting both mother and child. The pregnant woman who is using any kind of drugs, including tobacco and alcohol, should also talk to her doctor or nurse practitioner. With their medical advice and assistance, she can work out a safe and healthy plan to stop using drugs.

Just as soon as she stops, her body and her developing baby will begin to recover from the damaging effects. So no matter how long she has been pregnant, or how long she has been using, there are always benefits to stopping drug use.

Marijuana

Like tobacco, marijuana increases carbon monoxide levels in the mother's blood. Marijuana also has a direct effect on the mother's lungs, reducing the amount of oxygen that passes into her bloodstream. These factors combine to reduce the supply of oxygen available to the fetus, and may lower the infant's birthweight.

Cocaine and crack

When a pregnant woman uses cocaine, or crack, its smokable form, she causes her blood vessels to narrow and reduces the oxygen supply to the fetus. This increases her risk of having a low-birthweight baby who may also be at increased risk for sudden infant death syndrome (SIDS). She also increases the risk that her baby will be born prematurely. Cocaine use has been associated with heart defects, brain abnormalities, and other serious health problems.

Opiates

Opiates such as heroin pose very severe risks to the pregnant mother and her child. These risks include low birthweight, stillbirth, and death of the child soon after delivery (SIDS).

Babies exposed to heroin can have serious medical problems, which may include respiratory distress syndrome and seizures. They may also suffer from disturbed sleep patterns, vomiting and diarrhea, shaking and restlessness as a result of drug withdrawal. As they grow into children, they may have trouble learning and paying attention in school.

Amphetamines

Using amphetamines, including "crank" and "ice," during pregnancy increases the risk of miscarriage and may cause growth problems or heart and brain defects in the baby. Babies born to women who used amphetamines during pregnancy often suffer from tremors and rigid muscle tone and have trouble eating and sleeping.

Because amphetamines are often injected with needles, pregnant women who use them face another risk as well: the possibility of contracting HIV from an infected needle and passing it on to their babies.

It's never too late!

Many drugs interfere with a mother's capacity to be a good parent. If the mother is drug dependent, she may be more focused on her drug use than on her baby. Babies need mothers who can focus on them and provide sensitive and attentive care.

Remember, it is never too soon or too late to give up using drugs. Many woman have done it successfully. A pregnant or nursing woman who is using drugs and wants to quit should obtain medical help. A mentor's encouragement and her assistance in finding professional help can be invaluable.

Breastfeeding

One of the most important decisions a pregnant woman must make is whether or not to breastfeed her baby. This is a decision to think about and discuss before the baby is born.

Reasons to breastfeed

- Breast milk is always right for the baby. It is always the correct temperature and it is nutritionally perfect for human babies.

- Breast milk is the easiest milk for the baby to digest. Even the most expensive formula is not as good for the baby as breast milk. Babies who are breastfed have fewer digestive difficulties, spit up less often, and are less fussy.

- Breastfeeding helps prevent hemorrhaging associated with delivery. Breastfeeding causes the uterus to contract, and this helps reduce the flow of blood after delivery. This also helps the uterus to get back into shape more quickly after delivery.

- Breastfeeding promotes bonding between mother and baby.

- Breastfeeding exercises the baby's jaws and facial muscles more than bottle feeding. This exercise promotes proper development of the jaws, teeth, and face, and helps with speech development at a later age.

- Breastfed babies tend to have stronger immune systems than other babies. They are less prone to health problems such as allergies and respiratory and intestinal infections.

- The baby will not get too fat. You cannot overfeed a baby on breast milk alone. The mother's body always will produce the right amount of milk as long as she consistently breastfeeds the baby. Breastfed babies are more likely than bottle-fed babies to be of normal weight as children and as adults.

- Breast milk never needs any preparation.

- Traveling is easy because there are no bottles and formula to carry around.

- Night feedings are easy. Some mothers simply bring their hungry babies to bed and feed them there. Mothers who breastfeed tend to get more sleep than mothers who do not.

- Babies are less likely to be allergic to breast milk than to formulas.

- Breastfeeding mothers usually regain their figures more quickly and easily than mothers who do not breastfeed.

- Breast milk is all a baby needs to eat for the first four to six months after birth. It is nutritionally complete and meets all the baby's food needs.

- Breast milk is the most economical way to feed a baby. Formula is expensive. This expense is most often unnecessary, because breastfeeding is not only healthier, but also much cheaper. As long as the mother is reasonably healthy and eats a nutritionally complete diet, the breastfed baby is guaranteed the best nutrition available, regardless of the mother's financial status.

- If the mother tries breastfeeding and doesn't like it, she can always switch to using formula. However, if she starts with a formula, she cannot later switch to breastfeeding. This is why the decision to breast- or bottle-feed should be made before the baby is born.

- Even a few days of breastfeeding after birth will give the baby a head start. Before a mother's milk comes in, her breasts produce *colostrum,* a watery sweet substance that provides the baby with many important antibodies to fight infections. No formula can provide all the benefits of this special substance.

Some inconveniences of breastfeeding

- The mother must have a nutritionally sound diet. She must continue watching what she eats as long as she breastfeeds.

- In the beginning, other people cannot help with feeding the baby. Once the mother's milk supply is well established, though, she can start preparing bottles of her own milk so that others can feed the baby the mother's milk from these bottles.

- It is difficult to tell how much milk the baby has had. With a bottle, the mother knows how much she has fed her baby. However, as long as the baby is allowed to feed whenever she or he is hungry, the mother can assume that the baby is getting enough food. Regular checkups with the baby's doctor can reassure the mother.

- Breastfeeding involves a different life-style than bottle feeding. If the mother takes the baby out for longer than a few hours, she will have to decide whether or not she is willing to breastfeed in public. Some women feel very uncomfortable about this and choose to bottle-feed. Other women continue to breastfeed, but limit their public activities. It is an individual choice the mother has to make. However, having supportive friends and family can make it easier for a mother to choose to breastfeed.

- The mother's well-being is directly related to the baby's well-being. If the mother is ill, or exhausted, or not eating right, this will affect her milk supply. Bottle feeding does not depend so much on the mother's health. However, breastfeeding is often a good incentive for a young mother to take care of herself.

A warning about breastfeeding

If a mother is HIV positive, or thinks she may be, she should not breastfeed her baby. There is a chance that the virus could be passed on to the baby through the mother's milk.

Mothers who are breastfeeding must avoid tobacco, alcohol, and drugs, just as they did during pregnancy. See page 99 for more information.

The first feedings

For the first three or four days after birth, newborn babies do not need much food. What they do need during this time is the sweet watery substance that comes before the mother's milk comes in. This is exactly what a mother's breasts produce for the first few days after delivery. It is called *colostrum*.

Some new mothers worry that this substance is not real milk and wonder whether they are doing everything right. Colostrum is perfect for the newborn! Young mothers should know that their bodies are producing exactly what the baby needs at this stage of life. The real milk will come in a few days after birth. Until it does, the mother can be satisfied knowing she is giving her baby a very healthy substance that will provide valuable antibodies and nutrients.

Babies usually lose weight for four or five days after birth. After this time, most babies will start gaining weight. A new mother should not worry if her newborn is losing weight. Newborns do not eat much for the first few days after birth. In fact, a ten-day old baby will typically weigh the same as it did at birth.

The baby's sucking reflex

A hungry baby will turn its head toward a light touch or stroke on the cheek. When the mother is ready to feed the baby, she can stroke whichever cheek is closer to the breast, and the baby will turn its head toward her.

As the baby's head turns, the baby's lips will also purse. Then the mother can touch the baby's pursed lips with the nipple of her breast or a bottle, and the baby will latch on and begin to suck. All of these movements are part of the baby's sucking reflex, and they all begin with touching the baby's cheek that is closest to the mother's breast.

The nursing mother should avoid contradictory cues or cues that do not follow this order, as they may confuse the baby. For example, she should not touch both cheeks—the baby would not know which way to turn. Also, she should not touch the baby's lips first. The lips should be touched only after the cheek has been touched, the baby's head is turned, and the lips are pursed. The mother should have the nipple ready for the baby as soon as she stimulates the sucking reflex. Otherwise the baby will become frustrated at expecting food and not finding it immediately available.

Fears and frustrations

Many young mothers who are trying to breastfeed for the first time are easily discouraged. Starting to breastfeed is not easy. New mothers need to learn how to teach their babies to suck from the breast. Without support and encouragement, concerned young mothers often quit breastfeeding within the first week.

The first few days can be strange and uncomfortable. Mothers who breastfeed need a lot of support and information. Mothers with small breasts often worry about whether they will be able to produce enough milk. In fact, breast size is not related to milk production. Milk is produced in the glands behind the fatty tissue of the breast.

The mother's "real" milk takes a few days to come in. For the first few days after the baby's birth, the mother's breasts will be producing the watery sweet colostrum, perfectly suited for the baby's first few days. The mother's body will start producing the real milk just as soon as the baby is ready to digest it.

Breastfeeding doesn't come naturally to the mother or the baby! The new mother should not feel embarrassed or inadequate because breastfeeding doesn't feel natural or happen easily. Nurses often teach young mothers the basic techniques of breastfeeding. Some babies feed very easily, while others have to be taught or coaxed by their mothers. Nurses can also teach young mothers how to teach their babies to breastfeed.

Breastfeeding in the hospital is usually more difficult than breastfeeding at home. A hospital is a noisy, hectic place that tends to feel uncomfortable to both the mother and the baby. If the mother is frustrated with breastfeeding in the hospital, she should be encouraged not to give up. She'll probably find it much easier in the comfortable environment of her own home.

The let-down reflex

Sometimes a mother's breasts leak milk in response to her baby's cries, or even just in response to seeing her baby. The mother's body reacts to the baby by making the milk glands contract, and the contraction forces milk down into the milk ducts. This reaction is called the let-down or draft reflex.

This reflex is natural, and makes it easy for the baby to suck milk from the mother's breast. Sometimes, however, this reflex may make the mother uncomfortable, because she will find her breasts leaking milk at inconvenient times. Absorbent nursing pads or a clean handkerchief inside her bra can take care of this problem.

The supply and demand of breastfeeding

Many young mothers who are breastfeeding for the first time worry about whether their bodies will be able to make enough milk for their babies. A young mother should know that her breasts will automatically replace as much milk as the baby takes from her. The more milk the baby takes, the more milk the mother's body produces.

Breastfeeding is a natural supply and demand system that ensures there will always be enough milk, even as the baby grows and the need for milk increases. The system works perfectly as long as the baby is allowed to feed whenever she or he is hungry.

The mother should also make sure to feed the baby from both breasts at every feeding. The baby should empty both breasts. If the baby doesn't finish all the milk, the mother may have to express it by hand herself. The supply and demand system of breastfeeding works well only when the breasts are emptied of milk. It is the lack of milk in the breasts that causes the woman's body to produce more milk. If the breasts are not emptied at each feeding, the mother's body will not produce enough milk for the next feeding.

Expressing milk

Because the baby's eating habits may be unpredictable for the first few days, the mother's breasts may not always get emptied of milk. In this case, the mother should empty any leftover milk from her breasts so that her breasts will produce plenty of milk for the next feeding.

This process of getting rid of milk is called *expressing*. To express milk from her breasts, the mother will have to gently massage each breast with downward strokes toward the nipple. If the breast is fairly full, milk should be squirting out from the nipple. When the milk comes out in drops instead of streams, then the mother can stop expressing. She might want to express the milk into a sterile jar and then refrigerate it. If she wants, she can use it later to bottle feed the baby. It is important for the mother to know that her breasts will never be totally empty, because they are always producing milk.

Nutrition for the Nursing Mother ◆ ◆ ◆ ◆ ◆ ◆ ◆ ◆ ◆ ◆ ◆ ◆

Nursing mothers, like pregnant women, have to pay special attention to their diets. The nutrition of the nursing woman directly affects her baby. Generally, the nursing mother's nutritional intake should be much like her diet when she was pregnant. Certain foods and chemicals should be avoided, while others should definitely be included. Here are some basic nutrition hints.

Eat a variety of foods

Eating a variety of foods helps ensure that the mother and baby are getting all the different nutrients necessary for good health.

Eat natural foods

Generally, foods in their natural state are healthier than processed foods. Fresh foods are better than frozen or canned foods. Fruits and vegetables are especially good when they are fresh. This applies to raw as well as cooked fruits and vegetables. It is also wise to avoid foods that contain large amounts of preservatives. Processed foods tend to be high in these chemicals.

Drink lots of liquids

Nursing mothers naturally feel thirsty much of the time. To avoid the effects of dehydration, the nursing mother should drink plenty of water, fruit and vegetable juices, milk, and other liquids. She should avoid liquids containing caffeine, such as colas, coffee, and some kinds of tea. If the mother finds herself getting constipated or constantly thirsty, she should drink more liquids. She will know that she is getting plenty of fluids if her urine is a pale yellow color. If it's a dark yellow color, she should drink more liquids.

Get plenty of calcium

The nursing mother needs to be sure she is eating enough calcium-rich foods. Calcium will help give her and her baby strong bones. The most common source of calcium is cow's milk. However, some people are allergic to or dislike cow's milk, so they must find other foods from which to get their calcium. Other foods that are good sources of calcium are yogurt, hard cheeses such as cheddar and Swiss, and cottage cheese. Nondairy foods high in calcium are liver, canned sardines, almonds, cooked cabbage and collards, and sesame seeds. A nursing mother *does not* have to drink lots of milk for her body to make milk. If the mother is allergic to milk, or just doesn't like it, she can eat some of these other foods instead.

Restrict sugar and salt

Sugar tends to confuse the appetite. Sugary food falsely satisfies hunger and makes it less likely that you (and your baby) will get enough naturally nutritious food. People tend to feel full for a short time, after eating a lot of sugar, then crave more food—usually something else sugary. This can become an unhealthy nutritional cycle. The effects of sugar also include tooth decay.

Salt too is often overused. Too much salt can cause high blood pressure in the mother. Sugar and salt are both very common hidden ingredients in processed foods. Check the ingredient labels to avoid buying foods that are high in sugar and salt.

Restrict highly processed foods

Pre-sweetened cereal is an example of a highly processed food. Some cereals have little nutritional value and are very high in sugar. Young mothers should look for cereals and grains that are darker and coarser than the highly refined foods; for example, choose whole wheat or bran bread instead of white bread.

Beware a label that says the food has been "enriched." This usually means that the natural goodness of the food, such as fiber and nutrients, has been stripped away, then a few vitamins and minerals have been artificially added to the substandard product. This cannot take the place of the natural nutrients that have been removed.

Restrict caffeine

The nursing mother should restrict caffeine. This means avoiding coffee, tea, caffeinated sodas, and chocolate. If the breastfed baby gets too much caffeine, it can be fussy during the day and not gain weight quickly enough. If the mother is addicted to caffeine, she should try to cut back a little every day. If she drinks sodas or eats chocolate every day, or drinks more than three cups of coffee or tea a day, her caffeine intake is too high.

In general, a nursing mother should avoid the same things she avoided while she was pregnant. Here are some of the things to avoid while breastfeeding.

Some medications

The medications a woman avoided during pregnancy should also be avoided while breastfeeding. A mother who is breastfeeding should check with her doctor before taking any over-the-counter medications. And, if she receives prescription drugs from her doctor, she should be sure to tell the doctor that she is breastfeeding. The doctor can then ensure the drug is also safe for the baby.

Smoking

If the young mother stopped smoking during pregnancy, this is no time to start again. The effects of smoke on babies come from breathing the smoke as well as from drinking the mother's milk. Toxic substances from smoke are passed through the mother's bloodstream into her milk and eventually on to her baby.

A mother should not only avoid smoking, but also ask friends and relatives not to smoke near the baby or near other children. Babies who are exposed to smoke tend to have more respiratory illnesses, such as pneumonia and bronchitis.

Alcohol

Even small amounts of alcohol will affect the mother's milk. Nursing mothers should not drink alcoholic beverages.

Illegal drugs

Like tobacco and alcohol, drugs are passed on to the baby through the breast milk. Their use may interfere with milk production or with the baby's willingness to nurse, resulting in an inadequate milk supply. Nursing babies whose mothers use drugs tend to be irritable and jittery and have problems sleeping. Some of these problems may remain as they grow older.

Bottle Feeding Options ◆ ◆ ◆ ◆ ◆ ◆ ◆ ◆ ◆ ◆ ◆ ◆ ◆

Even the best formula is not as good for babies as the mother's own milk. However, if the new mother does not want to breastfeed or is not able to, she can use infant formula, which is also very good. There are some factors to consider when choosing and using formula.

Powdered formulas

Formula is least expensive in powdered form. Powdered formulas are light to carry and easy to store. However, they must be shaken up with the proper amount of water that has been boiled and cooled to the proper temperature. These formulas may be a good choice if the young mother does not have a refrigerator.

Liquid concentrates

These formulas are more expensive, heavier to carry, and need to be refrigerated after opening. However, they are easier to measure and to mix than the powdered formulas. Compared to powdered formulas, these are easier to use at home but more difficult when traveling.

Ready-mixed bottles

This is the most expensive type of formula to use. While the bottles are convenient and easy to use, because they come already mixed and sealed in presterilized disposable bottles, they are very expensive for everyday use.

Cow's milk

Cow's milk is made for calves. It is not good for very young babies. Compared to formula, cow's milk is too low in iron and too high in protein. It is also high in salt, which puts a strain on baby's kidneys. The new mother should not feed her baby any kind of cow's milk. She should use only specially made baby formulas.

Cleanliness

A new baby who is not breastfed is especially vulnerable to common germs. These germs, or bacteria, are everywhere. We carry them on our hands and our clothes, and we breathe them in all the time. Our adult bodies are able to defend themselves against illness from most of these germs, but a little baby's body is not as well prepared to resist infection. This is especially true when germs are in the milk the baby drinks.

Milk is an ideal breeding ground for germs, especially when kept at room temperature. A baby who drinks milk contaminated with bacteria can become quite ill with diarrhea and vomiting and rapidly become dehydrated.

Here are some tips for keeping the baby's milk as free as possible from germs:

- Wash hands before handling milk, and any time you use the bathroom or pet an animal.

- Use only sterilized formula. The cans of powder should be kept closed, and the cans of liquid should be covered. Once opened, liquid formula should be kept refrigerated.

- Sterilize everything used in measuring, mixing, or storing formula. This includes bottles, nipples, measuring spoons, mixing jars, and the water used to mix the formula. Water is sterile when it is boiled. The easiest way to sterilize feeding equipment is by submerging it in boiling water for 10 minutes. (Since some rubber nipples cannot be boiled, check the manufacturer's directions for nipple cleaning and sterilizing.)

These precautions should get rid of most of the germs. However, even if there are germs that haven't been killed, they cannot multiply too much while the milk is icy cold. It is the in-between temperatures that help bacteria grow and multiply. Here are some tips to help avoid these in-between temperatures:

- Cool the prepared milk quickly.

- Keep the formula cold until the baby wants it. Do not keep the milk warm for longer than a few minutes while the baby is not drinking it, even if the baby falls asleep during a feeding. Warm milk should *never* be put in a thermos or electric bottle warmer to be saved for later.

- Throw away any milk that the baby does not finish. Never try to save leftover formula for later. Obviously, leftover formula should not be poured back into the original container in the refrigerator.

Preparing powdered formula

A mother feeding her baby with powdered formula should mix the formula precisely according to the directions. She should measure the formula *only* with the scoop provided. Otherwise, she might not be using the correct amount, and the baby could either not get enough calories or get a diet that is too rich and hard to digest.

The water should be sterilized by boiling. The proper amount of water should be measured *after* it has been boiled. If it is measured before boiling, some water will evaporate during boiling, so she will not have the correct amount of water.

Here are the steps involved:

1. Boil water and let it cool to about body temperature.

2. Wash hands.

3. Pour the correct amount of water into the bottle or a sterilized jar. To make sure the amount is correct, put the container on a counter and look at it at eye level (not from above).

4. Add the right amount of milk powder. Use a knife to level off each scoop so it contains just the correct amount.

5. Stir water and powder with a sterile spoon, or cap the container and shake it vigorously.

6. Use the formula immediately (if making a single bottle) or pour it into sterile bottles, screw the nipples on upside down, and cover them with sterile caps.

Preparing liquid formula

As with powdered formula, the water should be boiled and then measured. Follow the instructions provided with the liquid formula.

Here are the basic steps:

1. Wash the top of the can under running water. This is to make sure that no dirt slips into the can when it is being opened.

2. Boil water to be mixed with formula.

3. Wash hands.

4. Pour boiled water over the top of the can to sterilize it.

5. Open the can and pour the liquid formula into sterile bottles. Add the correct amount of water, according to the instructions. Check to make sure the amounts are correct by putting the bottles on a counter and checking at eye level (not from above).

6. Cap bottles, cover jar if it is not emptied, and refrigerate.

7. Use refrigerated formula within 24 hours. The leftover liquid concentrate must also be covered and refrigerated. It will keep for longer than 24 hours (see package directions), but the mixed formula will not.

Note: *If the mother has no refrigerator, she must make each bottle individually, as needed. This is easiest if she is using a powdered mix that can be shaken up in the bottle. Without a refrigerator, it is NOT safe to prepare bottles that will not be used right away.*

There is a common myth that babies cry "to exercise their lungs." This is simply not true. Babies always cry for a reason. It is their way of communicating their different needs.

Parents are often frustrated when a baby cries and there seems to be no way to help the baby stop crying. In their frustration, parents are tempted to think that the baby will never stop crying. When this happens, it is important to remember that the baby cannot stop crying until its need is met. The trick, then, is to figure out what the baby needs.

Causes of crying

Hunger

This is the most common cause of crying for young babies. It is also the easiest need to satisfy. When a baby cries from hunger, it will only be satisfied by breast milk or formula. Fruit juices, sweetened water, or pacifiers will only stop the baby's crying temporarily. These will not satisfy the baby's need for nourishment.

Feeling cold

If a baby is awake, or almost awake, and feels chilly, the baby will cry. The crying will stop as soon as the baby is made comfortably warm.

Mothers often notice that their babies cry when taken outside. The change in temperature is often uncomfortable for the baby, and the baby needs extra warmth.

Need for contact

Babies often cry because they need physical contact and comfort. Sometimes the baby will cry after the parent has put it down. It is natural for the baby to be most satisfied when being held. Babies cry when they are deprived of contact comfort. If this is what the baby needs, then picking the baby up and cuddling it will stop the crying. Often, the most satisfying way to hold the baby is to have the baby's stomach and chest pressed close to the mother's body.

Many parents fear that picking up the baby every time the baby cries will lead to a spoiled child. However, young babies cannot become spoiled. Babies cry because they have some physical need that is not being met, and meeting this need is not spoiling. Babies do not make demands on parents (although a baby's crying may feel like a demand to the parent). Babies cry when they are deprived of something they need, including contact comfort.

Pain and discomfort

Babies cry when they experience pain. Common kinds of pain that babies experience include gas and other stomach discomfort, bottles and baths that are too hot, and being pricked by pins. Sometimes babies cry after feedings if they have not burped. Picking the baby up often leads to the baby burping or passing gas, and then the baby is comfortable again.

Some babies are more difficult to comfort than others. Their digestive systems are immature, and they have chronic gas pains for the first few months. These babies may not be happy unless they are held and walked. Mothers will be reassured to know that this condition won't last forever. Meanwhile, any of the numerous soft devices that keep the baby close to mother's body while leaving her hands free can be a godsend.

Too much stimulation

Babies will typically cry when they experience too much stimulation or very sudden stimulation that is unexpected. This can happen with loud noises, sudden bright lights, tickling, being touched by something cold or hot, or tasting something bitter. Babies also cry if they feel they are about to fall. Likewise, a baby may cry out of shock rather than out of real pain. For example, if a baby falls a short distance, the baby may cry from the shock of falling rather than from being hurt.

Being undressed

Babies like to feel warmth on their stomachs and chests. However, when a parent is changing the baby's diapers or clothes, the baby's stomach and chest may be left naked. Many babies cry from the loss of warmth and comfort they feel when their clothing is removed. An easy solution

to this discomfort is to put a small blanket, towel, or diaper across the baby's stomach and chest when the diaper is being changed. The warmth of the room might not have anything to do with the baby's crying. The baby just misses the contact of clothing on skin.

Twitching

Very young babies twitch and jerk as they begin to fall asleep. Sometimes this twitching and jerking startles the baby awake. When this happens, the baby will often cry for a moment and then become drowsy and fall asleep. Or the baby will twitch again and cry again and be unable to sleep soundly. An easy way to prevent the baby from being startled by its own movements is to securely wrap or swaddle the baby.

Ways to soothe the crying baby
Rhythm, movement, and sound

If everything else has been tried and the baby is clearly not hungry or in pain, then a constant rhythmical movement and sound will often soothe the crying baby.

Ways of soothing a baby include singing, playing music boxes, rocking, walking with the baby, and patting the baby on the back or the bottom.

Some innovative mothers find that running the vacuum cleaner, the dishwasher, or even a hair drier helps the baby. The rhythmical sounds seem to draw the baby's attention away from whatever is disturbing it. The best way to rock the baby seems to be to move the baby at a speed of more than 60 rocks per minute. Rocking the baby slower than that will often not help the baby stop crying. Therefore, if the baby is being rocked and is still crying, try rocking faster. It might work!

Sucking

As long as the baby is not hungry, sucking on a pacifier or the baby's own fingers will often soothe a crying baby. There is some controversy about whether or not to use pacifiers. Some babies don't need to be comforted with sucking, while others really do benefit from it. Perhaps the best advice is that the pacifier should not be used as a cure-all. Parents should make sure that the pacifier is not stuck in the baby's mouth every time the baby cries, because the baby may have other needs that are not being met.

A hungry baby will not be satisfied with a pacifier, nor will a baby who is in pain. The pacifier should probably be used as a last resort for a baby's crying. It is okay to use a pacifier if it soothes the baby, and if the parent guards against the baby becoming dependent on the pacifier as the baby's main source of comfort. Many babies will suck on their fingers rather than on a pacifier. Some babies find and suck on their fingers before they are born. Sometimes a parent can choose to comfort a baby by putting the baby's finger in its mouth as he or she is falling asleep.

Warmth

As mentioned before, babies crave warmth. If a baby seems to be crying for no apparent rea-son, the answer might be extra warmth. Rooms should generally be kept between 68 and 72 degrees Fahrenheit. However, a baby might want the additional warmth of being held or wrapped in a blanket. This is often true of babies who are waking up between feedings.

Swaddling

Many very young babies find it comforting to be wrapped securely, or swaddled. Others do not like it at all.

To swaddle a baby, lay the baby diagonally on a small blanket and wrap the left and right corners around the baby's body. Bend the baby's arms upward at the elbows and tuck them securely under the wrapping. (Older babies may prefer to have their arms free.) Finally, pull up the bottom corner of the blanket and tuck it securely into the folds of the blanket.

During the first few weeks after birth, the baby's sleeping and waking pattern is generally unpredictable. Babies will sleep as much as they need to, and when they are awake, it is usually because they don't need to sleep.

Although a mother has little control over the baby's sleeping schedule at this point, it is not too early to begin helping the baby differentiate between daytime and nighttime. Though the baby will sleep both during the day and at night, the mother can start helping the baby (and herself) sleep better at night in the future, when the baby's sleeping schedule becomes more regular.

All of the following suggestions are based on the mother treating the baby differently at night than in the daytime. When the baby is awake during the day, the mother can do things differently than when the baby wakes up at night. Likewise, when the baby sleeps during the day, the mother can treat this sleep differently than when the baby sleeps at night.

Putting the baby to bed

One of the first things a mother can do to help the baby learn the difference between night and day is to put the baby to bed every time the baby sleeps. Even when the baby is just napping, putting the baby in the crib or carriage will soon help to associate these places with sleep. It is also important to get the baby up from the crib or carriage when the baby wakes, especially during the day.

Letting the baby hear normal household noises

Another way to help the baby distinguish daytime from nighttime is to carry on with normal activities during the day, even when the baby is sleeping. Many new parents try to be very quiet whenever the baby is sleeping, even during the day. However, if the baby needs to sleep, normal household noises will not keep it from sleeping. Eventually, the baby will learn to associate the noisiness of the day with being awake, and the quiet of the night with being asleep.

During the day
Keep the baby out of the bedroom
During the day, it is important to keep the baby in the center of family activity. Whether the baby is kept in the kitchen or the living room, or moved around, the baby will learn to associate activity with daytime and wakefulness. Likewise, the baby will learn to associate being put to bed in the bedroom with nighttime and sleepiness.

Keep the baby stimulated
When the baby is awake during the day, provide a comfortable amount of stimulation. Babies like and need to look at bright colors, big pat-

terns, and moving objects. They also like to hear pleasant sounds. Playing with a baby by showing the baby different toys might not seem like a lot of activity, but to a baby this kind of play can be very stimulating and tiring. Keeping the baby stimulated during the day will help to associate the daytime with fun activities.

Take the baby outside

In the early weeks, the mother can place the baby near a window for part of the day. When the baby gets older, she can start with short excursions. As long as weather conditions are not extreme, it is good for babies to spend time outside in fresh air. Taking the baby outside during the day is a stimulating activity. The baby will enjoy the many different sights, sounds, and feelings of the outdoors.

During the night

Avoid stimulation

One way to help the baby sleep well at night is to avoid stimulation when the baby is awake. If the baby needs to be changed or fed at night, avoid turning on lights and talking a lot. The mother should not chat too much with the baby or offer toys. The trick is to make the baby's wakeful time at night as boring and unstimulating as possible. One may want to keep a hallway light or a night light on near the baby's room. This way, when the baby needs to be fed or changed at night, there's no need to turn on a bright light.

Make the baby's room darker

Although the mother may want a little light in the baby's room at night, the room should be darker at night than during the day. A dark room at night will help the baby associate darkness with nighttime and sleep. Also, in a darkened room, the baby will not be able to look at all the interesting things that might otherwise entertain the baby during the daytime.

Make the baby comfortable

Babies often wake up when they are uncomfortable. Babies get uncomfortable when they are hungry or cold or when they have gas. When putting the baby to bed, a mother can make the baby comfortable by feeding and burping and by making sure the baby is warm enough. If the baby is wrapped at night, its own movements, such as twitching and jerking, will be less likely to awaken it.

A warning about sleep positions

Sometimes babies die in their sleep for no apparent reason. Although no one knows exactly why or how this happens, scientists have learned that babies who sleep on their stomachs are more susceptible to sudden infant death syndrome (SIDS, or crib death). The U.S. Surgeon General therefore recommends that babies be put to sleep on their sides instead of on their stomachs.

Starting Solid Foods ◆ ◆ ◆ ◆ ◆ ◆ ◆ ◆ ◆ ◆ ◆ ◆ ◆ ◆ ◆

There is much disagreement about when to start feeding a baby solid foods. In general, babies should not be fed solid foods until they are developmentally ready for them—usually between four and six months of age. Until that time, babies receive all the nutrition they need from the mother's milk or infant formula.

There are good reasons why a baby should not be fed solid foods before the age of four to six months. One reason is that very young babies cannot easily digest anything solid. Feeding solid foods in the early months will often cause stomach upsets or even provoke allergic reactions.

This is especially true of cow's milk and other dairy products. These foods are less likely to cause problems if they are given at six months or older.

Here are some hints for knowing when and how to start feeding the baby solid foods:

- The baby's mouth movements have matured, so the tongue no longer reflexively pushes everything back out of the mouth. As babies start to teethe they develop a natural urge to chew and bite. This means that the baby's tongue, mouth, and digestive system are preparing for solid foods.

- The baby has a bigger appetite than milk can satisfy. When the baby still seems hungry and demands more food, even after the mother has increased the frequency of feedings for four or five days, the time for starting solid foods may have arrived.

- By the time most babies are ready for solid foods, they are able to hold their heads up well and sit up alone in a high chair. At this time, they naturally start reaching for things and want to put everything into their mouths.

How to introduce solid foods

When starting with solid foods, it is important to remember that the baby will get a better start if new foods are introduced slowly. Solid foods should not immediately replace the breast or bottle. It will be healthier for the baby, and much easier for the mother, if the transition to solid foods is started slowly and continues gradually.

- The easiest way to begin feeding solid foods is to have the baby sit in its chair or in the mother's lap.

- The baby should be breast- or bottle-fed briefly first, before being given solid food.

This will help take the edge off the baby's hunger, and the baby will be in a better mood. Solid foods should not be introduced while a baby is cranky.

- The first few introductions to solid food should not constitute a full meal for the baby. The purpose is to get the baby used to new kinds of food.

- If the baby does not seem to like eating from the spoon, try putting a dab of food on the feeding tray for baby to explore. The main idea is to let the baby get used to new kinds of food. Spoons can be introduced later.

- Start the first day of solid food with only about a quarter of a teaspoon of the food. Increase the amount of that same food the next day. Over the space of a week, keep increasing the amount of that food, until by the end of the week the baby is getting as much as it wants two or three times a day.

- Give the baby only as much food as it wants. A baby who does not want more food will let the parent know by spitting it out, turning away, or shutting its mouth. Forcing the baby to eat can start feeding problems that last a long time.

- Introduce new foods slowly. It is good if the baby is given a new food about once a week. Baby does not need to have a variety of solid foods all at once. One good reason for giving the baby only one new food at a time is to watch for allergic reactions. If the baby develops a rash or a sore bottom, it is probably having an allergic reaction to the new food.

- Once a new food has been introduced, try to keep at least a little bit of it on the baby's menu once a week during the baby's first year. This will help avoid a possible allergic reaction if the food is reintroduced much later.

- Do not be too concerned about neatness during the early stages of feeding solid foods. The important thing is to get the baby to eat solid foods, not to be perfectly neat.

- One way to contain the mess is to have only one thing at a time on the baby's tray. Not only does this help keep the eating area cleaner, but it also makes it easier for the baby to concentrate on that one thing. Keeping only one thing at a time in front of the baby is a good idea whether it is a piece of finger food, a single unbreakable dish with one food in it, or a small unbreakable cup. Keep the servings small.

- To avoid choking, never, never give grapes, peanuts, hard candy, or other small, firm pieces of food to a baby or a young child. And never leave the baby alone during feeding time, even for a minute, while you are introducing solid foods.

Choosing the first solid foods

There are advantages and disadvantages to both homemade and store-bought baby foods. Commercial foods are easy to serve and the perfect consistency for beginning eaters, but they can be expensive. Although most commercial baby foods do not contain artificial ingredients, it is still wise to read labels and avoid those with added salt and sugar, artificial flavorings, and preservatives.

The consistency that makes these foods ideal for infants is a disadvantage when the child grows a little older and can handle chunky foods. Babies who are fed exclusively store-bought foods even as they grow older become accustomed to the soft texture and may have difficulty adjusting to the varied textures of the family's table food.

Homemade baby foods, prepared with a blender, a food processor, or even just a fork, take time, but save money. They also give the mother greater control over what her baby eats. If you plan to serve table food to the baby, put her or his portion aside before adding spices, sugar, salt, or fat. Steam or pressure cook vegetables to retain their nutrients. As the baby grows older, many foods can be mashed or chopped rather than pureed.

Check with the baby's doctor for suggested first foods. Many doctors recommend the following sequence:

- *Rice cereal.* The American Academy of Pediatricians recommends rice cereal as baby's first solid food. Rice cereal is unlikely to cause allergic reactions, and is prepared for babies with added iron. Powdered cereals may be mixed with breast milk, formula, or water to whatever consistency is appropriate for the baby's stage of development, starting with a very thin mixture and gradually increasing the amount of cereal. After rice cereal, oatmeal and perhaps barley may be added. Because some babies are allergic to wheat, it is usually not one of the first foods offered.

- *Vegetables.* Vegetables have a stronger taste than cereals, but most babies find them interesting. If they are offered before fruits, babies may be less likely to reject tastes that are not sweet. Cook and puree them at first, then mash them as the baby gets older. When the time for finger foods arrives, offer chunks of cooked vegetables that are easy to hold. Cooked carrots, potatoes, and sweet potatoes are especially popular. Some raw vegetables, such as carrots and celery, can be a choking hazard. Grated raw carrots are a safe and tasty treat.

- *Fruits.* Babies love ripe bananas. Start by mashing up a little bit of banana with a fork, then gradually offering unmashed pieces of banana. Raw apples and peeled pears may be grated, or scraped with the edge of a spoon, so baby can be given a little pile of the fruit on the feeding table or tray. Once the baby is older, small pieces of peeled apple or pear are fine as finger food. Babies love the flavor and the crunchiness. Pieces of chilled fruit can even relieve the discomfort of teething. Citrus fruits and their juices are best postponed, since some babies are allergic to them.

- *Meat.* Meats are usually introduced after vegetables and fruits. Like these foods, they are usually pureed at first and only gradually offered mashed or chopped. Fish is best postponed, since allergies are not uncommon. If you do give a baby fish, be sure all bones have been removed. Avoid breaded frozen fish, which is high in fat and low in protein.

- *Breads, biscuits, and crackers.* Babies enjoy eating pieces of dried or toasted bread as finger foods. Whole grain breads are more nutritious than white bread. Teething babies especially love dry biscuits and toast. Avoid commercial crackers made for adults that are high in fat and salt.

- *Eggs.* Eggs should not be introduced until the baby is about one year old. Many babies have allergic reactions to eggs, especially when the eggs are introduced too early. When the baby is about a year old, pieces of cut up hard-boiled egg make a great finger food. Most babies also enjoy scrambled eggs.

- *Cow's milk and dairy products.* The only milk a baby actually needs is the mother's milk or formula. Many babies develop allergies to cow's milk, so it is best to avoid giving cow's milk to a young baby. Cottage cheese, yogurt, and other cheeses can be introduced at around nine or 10 months of age. These dairy products are less likely to cause allergies than cow's milk. They are also a good source of calcium.

When to Call the Doctor

A mother should not hesitate to call her doctor or health care provider whenever she notices a sudden change in the baby's routine or behavior. It never hurts to ask questions. Call for help whenever the baby:

- has no appetite and is not taking fluids
- sleeps more than usual and can't be awakened easily
- is unusually cranky or fussy and can't be comforted
- is having trouble breathing
- has diarrhea (very loose, watery, bad-smelling stools more than three times a day)
- has a dry diaper serveral hours after the last change
- is vomiting
- has a fever, feels hot, or looks flushed. (A fever is a rectal temperature of 101° F or higher in a baby under three months or 102° F in a baby over four months.)
- takes medicine for a fever, but it still doesn't go down
- seems weak and doesn't have the energy to cry as loudly as usual
- seems to have an earache or a stiff neck, or pulls at the ears

The Baby's Development

Each baby is unique and special, and different from any other baby. Children grow and develop at different rates. The following section describes *general* growth and maturation patterns for babies and young children. Remember that these are general patterns, and any given baby may be a little faster or slower than the patterns described here. This is not a cause for alarm. If a young mother is concerned about her baby's development, however, she should consult a health care provider.

Newborn

Newborn babies do little else but sleep. A newborn baby's eyes will respond to bright light. The pupils will dilate and the baby may close its eyes.

1 Month

At one month old, a baby still does very little but sleep and eat. The baby who is one month old may be able to follow an object with its eyes for just a brief amount of time.

3 Months

By three months of age, babies have gained coordination and generally spend more time awake. A baby begins to do the following at three months:

- brings hands together above body while lying on back
- holds rattle for a short time
- turns head towards a sound
- coos and smiles

6 Months

At six months of age, a baby is much stronger and more coordinated than at birth. Babies of this age stay awake even longer, and have more need for stimulation and play. A baby begins to do the following at six months:

- smiles and makes responsive noises
- makes singsong noises and two-syllable sounds, such as a-da or a-a
- screams if annoyed or irritated
- can lift head
- sits with or without support
- rolls over
- holds up arms to be lifted
- grasps toys
- brings everything to the mouth
- shakes and watches a rattle

9 Months

At nine months of age, a baby begins to do the following:

- sits up, might be able to start crawling

- can pull itself up briefly
- uses finger to poke and point
- babbles a lot
- shouts for attention
- might copy adult noises like coughs and laughs
- can hold, bite, and chew a cookie or teething biscuit

1 Year (12 Months)

At one year of age, a baby will be able to do the following:

- sits up well
- crawls or shuffles
- pulls up to standing position
- might be able to briefly walk or stand
- drops and throws toys
- holds spoon, but can't use it
- waves bye-bye
- recognizes people
- might notice pictures
- likes company and playing

1 1/2 Years (18 Months)

At the age of 18 months, a baby can do the following:

- walks easily
- can crawl on stairs
- can run, but stares at the ground

- likes holding or clutching teddy bears or other stuffed animals
- likes picture books
- can scribble
- points to eyes, nose, ears, hair, and other body parts
- says six to 20 words, but understands more than that number
- tries singing
- can use a spoon
- drinks from cup, but spills
- may be able to control bowels, but not bladder—still wets

2 Years (24 Months)

At two years of age, a child probably:

- runs easily, but leans forward when running
- finishes teething, cuts the last baby teeth
- turns pages in a book
- talks to herself or himself
- can say short sentences
- obeys simple commands
- spoon-feeds self and drinks from a cup
- asks for food, drink, and maybe the toilet
- throws tantrums

About Toilet Training ◆ ◆ ◆ ◆ ◆ ◆ ◆ ◆ ◆ ◆ ◆ ◆ ◆ ◆

The following is a brief description of the stages in toilet training. Different children start toilet training at different ages. These, again, are just general indications. If a child is slightly ahead of or behind these general stages, it is probably not a cause for concern. This is a general outline.

1 Year

At one year of age, a baby has no control over its bowel movements or bladder.

1 Year, 3 Months (15 Months)

At 15 months of age, a baby may be able to tell its mother about a bowel movement or urination *after* it has happened.

1 Year, 6 Months (18 Months)

At 18 months of age, a baby is still unable to control a bowel movement or urination before it occurs. However, the toddler may be able to tell just at the time that the bowel movement or urination is happening, whereas at 15 months, the report came after it had already happened.

1 Year, 9 Months (21 Months)

At 21 months of age, a baby may be able to tell in time for the mother to get him or her to the bathroom.

2 Years (24 Months)

At 2 years of age, a young child can tell its mother in time to get to the bathroom for urination.

2 Years, 3 Months (27 Months)

At this age, a young child may be able to stay clean and dry during the day. At night, the child may not be able to control its bowel and bladder.

2 Years, 6 Months (30 Months)

At this age, the young child should be able to stay clean and dry during the day, and may also be gaining control over its bowels and bladder at night.

2 Years, 9 Months (33 Months)

At this age, the child may be able to remain clean and dry during the day and night. However, there may still be occasional accidents with wetting.

3 Years (36 Months)

By three years of age, a child should be able to stay clean and dry during the day and at night.

Facts and Fictions about HIV/AIDS ◆ ◆ ◆ ◆ ◆ ◆ ◆ ◆ ◆ ◆ ◆

Myth: *AIDS is a disease of gay, white males.*

Fact: *AIDS affects homosexuals and hetero-sexuals; it affects men, women, and children.*

- In 1992, new AIDS cases were up 9% among women, but only 2.5% among men.

- African Americans are 12% of the population, but 32% of people with AIDS. Latinos are 9% of the population, but 17% of people with AIDS.

- Among African American people with AIDS, 22% are women.

- Among women with AIDS, 54% are African American. AIDS cases have occurred 14 times more frequently among black women than among white women.

- Of all children with AIDS, 55% are African American, 24% are Latino, and 20% are Caucasian.

The best way to fight AIDS is to know the facts and to think before you act. Here are the facts about AIDS.

What is AIDS?

AIDS is the last stage of a fatal disease caused by the Human Immunodeficiency Virus, or HIV. HIV causes a breakdown in the immune system, the body's defense against diseases and infections.

Without a healthy immune system to fight off sickness, people with HIV are prone to all kinds of other diseases and infections. At this time there is no vaccine against HIV and no cure for it, although some medications may slow its course. Having HIV ultimately results in AIDS and death.

Who can get AIDS?

Anyone can get AIDS. Who you are doesn't matter—what you do does. People who engage in high-risk behaviors, such as injecting drugs or having unprotected sex, especially with a number of different partners, are at great risk for contracting HIV.

How do people get AIDS?

HIV disease may be contracted only through the exchange of bodily fluids—blood, semen, vaginal secretions, and breast milk. There are two primary ways that this may occur: during unprotected sex with an infected individual and through using needles or syringes previously used by an infected individual. Mothers who are HIV positive have babies who also test positive for HIV when they are born. However, most of these children will not remain HIV positive.

Through vaginal, anal, or oral sex

If your sexual partner is infected with HIV, then you are in danger of getting it. The virus may enter the bloodstream through cuts or sores on the penis, in the rectum or vagina, or in the mouth. Sometimes these are cuts or sores so small that you are not even aware they are there. Even so, if blood, semen, or vaginal secretions from an infected person comes in contact with them, the chances of becoming infected with HIV disease are high. HIV may be passed from male to male, from male to female, from female to male, and from female to female.

By sharing needles or syringes

People who inject intravenous (IV) drugs and share needles or syringes, even once, are in grave danger of contracting HIV. This is because blood left in the needle or syringe from the first person will be injected directly into the bloodstream of the second person. When the first person is a carrier of HIV, the second person will also become infected.

Needles used to inject street drugs or steroids may carry HIV. Even needles used for tattooing or ear piercing can transmit HIV, so be sure to go to a qualified technician for these services—and be sure the needles have been sterilized before they are used.

Through prenatal exposure

One other way to get HIV is to be born with it. If a woman is infected with HIV disease before or during her pregnancy, there is a 25% (1 in 4) chance that she will pass the virus on to her baby. This can occur during the pregnancy, during the birth of the child, or during breastfeeding. Mothers who know or suspect that they are HIV positive should not breastfeed their babies.

Men and Women and AIDS ◆ ◆ ◆ ◆ ◆ ◆ ◆ ◆ ◆ ◆ ◆ ◆ ◆ ◆

About men

- Men who have sex with other men account for a large proportion (62%) of all AIDS cases. In the Caucasian population, the majority of men with AIDS (78%) contracted it through having sex with other men.

- Intravenous (IV) drug use is responsible for 25% of all AIDS cases, 37% of AIDS cases in African American men, and 38% of cases in Latino men.

- Men who have sex with other men and also inject drugs account for 7% of all cases.

- Only a small percentage (7%) of all AIDS cases in men come from heterosexual sex.

About women

- Intravenous (IV) drug use accounts for the greatest percentage of AIDS cases among women (49%). The percentage of women who get AIDS through heterosexual sex has been increasing every year, especially among African American and Latino women.

- Heterosexual sex accounts for a large percentage of AIDS cases among women (35%).

- Ten percent of HIV cases among women come from an unknown source. This means that their sexual partners may have engaged in IV drug use or unprotected sex without the women's knowledge. They may not even have known that they were carrying HIV. The fact that so many women do not know how they were infected underlines the importance of precautions for women.

Risky Behaviors

Certain behaviors put people at high risk for getting HIV/AIDS.

- Sharing drug needles or syringes

- Having anal, oral, or vaginal sex without a latex condom (unprotected sex) with an infected person

- Having unprotected sex with someone who shoots drugs

- Having unprotected sex with someone you don't know well (a pickup or prostitute) or with someone who you know has had numerous sex partners. Unprotected sex is *always* a risk.

Safe Behaviors

- Not having sex

- Not shooting drugs
- Having sex only with one faithful, uninfected partner
- Using a latex condom consistently and correctly when having sex

How do you know if someone has AIDS or HIV?

The answer is you don't know—so you should never take chances and assume it's OK. People infected with HIV may have no symptoms for up to 10 years, although some become ill soon after they come in contact with the virus. Many people don't even know they are infected. You can't tell by looking at a person if he or she is carrying HIV.

AIDS and the Single Woman

Getting to know other people is a normal part of life, especially for young adults. Sometimes friendship leads to sex. Since your partner has been sexually active, it is important for her to know that unprotected sex involves serious risks, whether it is vaginal, oral, or anal. The biggest risk related to these behaviors is AIDS.

Be sure your partner understands that there is no foolproof way of knowing if anyone she meets has been exposed to HIV. As long as she avoids sexual activity and sharing drug needles, she will probably not have to worry about HIV. If she is sexually active, encourage her to ask these difficult but important questions early in each new relationship:

- Have you had any sexually transmitted diseases?

- Have you had unprotected oral, anal, or vaginal sex with anyone who may have been infected with HIV?

- Have you experimented with drugs, or been a regular user?

- Have you shared needles or syringes to inject drugs or steroids?

- Did you receive blood transfusions or blood products between 1978 and 1985?

- Have you ever tested positive for HIV?

These are sensitive and difficult questions to ask, but remind your partner that if she knows someone well enough to have sex, she should know them well enough to talk about AIDS. If someone is unwilling to talk about sex and AIDS, she should not have sex with this person. And if the person answers yes to any of the above questions, that person should be tested for HIV, and your partner should not engage in sexual activity with this person until the results from the tests are known. Also, if your partner answers yes to any of these questions, she should consider being tested for HIV.

If your partner is sexually active, the safest way she can continue to be sexually active is to use latex condoms, or rubbers, correctly every time she has sex, no matter how well she may think she knows someone. She needs to use them every time she has sex, from start to finish. That includes oral and anal sex.

Pregnant Women and HIV/AIDS

If your partner thinks she may be HIV positive, encourage her to be tested as soon as possible. A pregnant woman who is HIV positive should look into the possibility of receiving AZT, a drug that can prolong life and minimize the effects of AIDS. It may also protect her baby from HIV.

In 1994, dramatic results were announced from a program that gave AZT to HIV-positive women in the last two trimesters of pregnancy and during birth, then to the baby early in its life. The infants' risk of testing positive was reduced by 67%.

Pregnant women who are HIV positive are eligible to receive AZT through Medicaid. If the woman is under 18 years of age she may not have to pay for the medication. When a woman is not eligible for Medicaid or the assistance is inadequate, mentors may be able to find help through organizations with which they are affiliated. The potential benefit to the infant is great.

If a woman has already had her baby, but tests positive for HIV, she is still eligible to receive AZT through Medicaid. HIV-positive Medicaid recipients in every state are eligible to receive AZT.

Condoms Help Prevent AIDS

◆ ◆ ◆ ◆ ◆ ◆ ◆ ◆ ◆ ◆ ◆ ◆

The information on this sheet can save your partner's life. Please pass it on to her in any way you can.

The most effective strategy to protect yourself against AIDS (besides avoiding the risky behaviors already mentioned) is to use a latex condom or "rubber" correctly whenever you have sex. In order for condoms to be effective, you must use a new one every time you have sex—from start to finish. The Surgeon General has issued specific recommendations about condom use.

- Use *latex* rubber condoms. "Lambskin" or "natural membrane" condoms made of porous materials are not effective in protecting against HIV. Look for the words *latex* or *disease prevention* on the package.

- Always use a *water-based* lubricant if the condom is not pre-lubricated. This makes it less likely that irritation, such as scratching or scraping, will occur, and also less likely that the condom will break. Spermicide can act as a lubricant. A surgical lubricant or K-Y Jelly™ may also be used. You can tell if the lubricant is water based (water soluble) by reading the writing on the package.

- Use a *new* condom every time you have vaginal, oral, or anal sex.

- Warn your partner not to use petroleum jelly (Vaseline™), cold cream, hand or body lotions, cooking oil, or baby oil. These products can weaken the rubber and cause the condom to break. For a free brochure on how to use a condom correctly, call the AIDS Clearinghouse at 800/342-AIDS. The brochure is available in English and in Spanish.

Why do condoms protect against AIDS?

Condoms act as a barrier against semen, blood, and vaginal fluids. Since HIV cannot be passed on (except from mother to child) without the exchange of one of these fluids, condoms can block the passage of the virus.

Other benefits of using condoms

Using condoms will also protect your partner against other sexually transmitted diseases, such as chlamydia, herpes simplex virus, genital ulcers, gonorrhea, hepatitis B, and pelvic inflammatory disease. And of course, using condoms also protects against pregnancy.

Condoms are not 100% safe—but if used correctly and consistently, they will greatly reduce the risk of becoming infected with HIV.

Alcohol, Drugs, and AIDS ◆ ◆ ◆ ◆ ◆ ◆ ◆ ◆ ◆ ◆ ◆ ◆ ◆ ◆

Teenagers and young adults are at the age when trying new things is especially inviting. Alcohol and drugs may be particularly attractive to young people. Although alcohol and drugs do not cause AIDS, people who use them increase their risk of becoming infected with HIV.

Here are some facts:

- Many people who become infected with HIV are heroin, cocaine, or speed users who use needles to shoot, or inject, drugs.

- Sharing needles passes HIV directly from the bloodstream of one person to that of another. Blood from an infected person can be trapped in the needle or syringe, and then injected straight into the bloodstream of the next person who uses the needle. This is the most direct way to spread HIV.

- When people are under the influence of alcohol and drugs they sometimes do things that they would not do if they weren't high. Every day, people are killed in car accidents because they were driving drunk or high. When we're sober, almost all of us know that driving under the influence of alcohol or other drugs is dangerous and life-threatening behavior. Like-

wise, people know that having sex without condoms is how HIV is spread. But, when people are on drugs and alcohol, they are much less likely to use condoms.

- Drugs and alcohol are harmful to the body. They hurt the body and cause damage to the immune system, which helps the body fight disease. The more alcohol and drugs a person uses, the worse the effects are on the body.

- Drugs and alcohol are expensive and highly addictive. People who are addicted to these substances are often reduced to prostitution in order to satisfy their body's craving. This puts them at extremely high risk for contracting and transmitting HIV.

Just using drugs or drinking alcohol does not mean that a person will get AIDS. But it is important to be aware that using drugs and alcohol may easily lead to unsafe sex and sharing needles.

Ways You Can't Get AIDS ◆ ◆ ◆ ◆ ◆ ◆ ◆ ◆ ◆ ◆ ◆ ◆ ◆

People worry about a lot of ways they might get AIDS. Here are the ways you *won't* get AIDS.

- Casual contact, just being around a person with HIV
- Sneezes and coughs
- Contact with items that an infected person has used or touched, such as:

  –drinking glasses

  –silverware

  –telephones

  –toilet seats

  –doorknobs
- Mosquito bites or bites from other bugs
- Sweat, tears, urine, or a bowel movement
- Giving blood
- Swimming in a pool with someone with HIV
- Kissing
- Hugging

The bottom line is: If there is no exchange of blood, semen, or vaginal fluids (or, in the case of infants, breast milk), there is no danger of HIV transmission.

A note about giving blood

You never get AIDS from giving blood. The needles are used only once and then destroyed. Giving blood is completely safe.

In the past, people have gotten AIDS through *getting* blood. Since 1985, however, all blood donors have been screened and all blood has been tested for HIV. This has virtually eliminated the possibility of getting AIDS from blood transfusions.

For further information

If you or your partner have more questions about AIDS or HIV, you can call the National AIDS Hotline at 800/342-AIDS. You don't have to give your name, and the people there can answer most any question you may have.

Sources and Resources ◆ ◆ ◆ ◆ ◆ ◆ ◆ ◆ ◆ ◆ ◆ ◆ ◆ ◆

What Pregnant Woman Should Know

American Council for Drug Education. (1991). *Drugs and pregnancy: It's not worth the risk.* Rockville, MD: American Council for Drug Education.

Brown, J. E. (1983). *Nutrition for your pregnancy.* Minneapolis: University of Minnesota Press.

Eisenberg, A., Murkoff, H. E., and Hathaway, S. E. (1991). *What to Expect When You're Expecting.* New York: Workman Publishing.

Fetal Alcohol Syndrome Work Group. (1986). *For your baby's sake, don't drink.* Chicago: Illinois Department of Alcoholism and Substance Abuse.

Krauss, M., Castle, S., & Lunden, J. (1988). *Your newborn baby: Everything you need to know.* New York: Warner Books.

La Leche League International (1991). *The womanly art of breastfeeding* (35th ed.). New York: Plume Printing.

Leach, P. (1989). *Your baby and child: From birth to age five.* (Rev. ed.). New York: Alfred A. Knopf.

National Clearinghouse for Alcohol and Drug Information (NCADI). (1985). *Fetal alcohol syndrome.* Rockville, MD: NCADI.

National Clearinghouse for Alcohol and Drug Information (NCADI). (1989). *The fact is ... Alcohol and other drugs can harm an unborn baby.* Rockville, MD: NCADI.

Nilsson, L. (1990). *A Child Is Born.* Text by Lars Hamberger. New York: Delacorte.

Office for Substance Abuse Prevention (OSAP). (1991). *How to take care of your baby before birth.* Rockville, MD: OSAP.

Rinzler, C. A. (1984). *The safe pregnancy book.* New York: New American Library.

Shaw, R. (1991). "Exercise: How much? How often?" *Baby on the Way 2:* 14–16.

U.S. Department of Agriculture. (1990). *Pregnant? Drugs and alcohol can hurt your unborn baby.* Washington, DC: General Printing Office.

von Nostitz, P. (1991). "What type of exercise is best for you?" *Expecting 24:* 22-30, 74-75.

After the Baby Is Born

Brazelton, T. B. (1992). *Touchpoints: Your child's emotional and behavioral development.* Reading, MA: Addison-Wesley.

Eisenberg, A., Murkoff, H. E., & Hathaway, S. E. (1989). *What to expect the first year.* New York: Workman Publishing.

Krauss, M.; Castle, S.; & Lunden, J. (1988). *Your newborn baby: Everything you need to know.* New York: Warner Books.

La Leche League International. (1991). *The womanly art of breastfeeding* (35th ed.). New York: Plume Printing.

Leach, P. (1989). *Your baby and child: From birth to age five.* New York: Alfred A. Knopf.

Leach, P. (1990). *Your growing child*. New York: Alfred A. Knopf.

Leach, P. (1993). *Your baby and child*. New York: Alfred A. Knopf.

Lief, Nina R. (1991). *The first year of life*. New York: Walker and Company.

Sears, W., and Sears, M. (1992). *The baby book: Everything you need to know about your baby from birth to age two*. Boston, MA: Little Brown.

Spock, B., & Rothenberg, M. B. (1992). *Dr. Spock's baby and child care*. New York: Pocket Books.

HIV and AIDS

American Red Cross (ARC). (1992). *Children, parents and HIV*. Washington, DC: ARC. Call your local Red Cross chapter or 202/973-6000.

Centers for Disease Control and Prevention. (1990). *Voluntary HIV counseling and testing: Facts, issues, and answers*. Rockville, MD: U.S. Department of Health and Human Services.

Centers for Disease Control and Prevention National AIDS Clearinghouse and National Pediatric HIV Resource Center. (January 1994). *HIV/AIDS and adolescents: Educational materials*. Call either 800/362-0071 or 800/458-5231 for this free annotated bibliography.

Child Welfare League of America (CWLA). (1991). *Adolescents: At Risk for HIV Infection*. Washington, DC: CWLA. A video for people who work with at-risk teens. Order by calling 908/225-1900 and asking for stock # 4549.

ETR Associates. (1994). Think About It Brochures: *Abstinence, Condoms, STDs, HIV,* and *Drugs*. Santa Cruz, CA: ETR Associates. Individual brochures with parallel English and Spanish text. Call 800/321-4407 or write ETR Associates, PO Box 1830, Santa Cruz, CA 95061-1830.

National AIDS Hotline. Call 800/342-AIDS.

Rahlev, Mary C., and Riley, Martha. (1993). *Youth and HIV: It's up to you and me*. Washington, DC: Project CHAMP, Children's National Medical Center. Call 202/884-5450 or write to Project CHAMP, Children's National Medical Center, 111 Michigan Avenue NW, Washington, DC 20010.

San Francisco AIDS Foundation. (1990). *Alcohol, drugs, & AIDS*. San Francisco, CA: San Francisco AIDS Foundation.

Surgeon General & Centers for Disease Control. (1991). *America responds to AIDS: Understanding AIDS*. Rockville, MD: U.S. Department of Health and Human Services.